THE
BREAKING
POINT

THE BREAKING POINT

UNDERSTANDING YOUR POTENTIAL FOR VIOLENCE

NICHOLAS REGUSH

KEY PORTER BOOKS

Canadian Cataloguing in Publication Data

Regush, Nicholas M., 1946–

  The breaking point : understanding your potential for violence

ISBN 1-55013-836-7

1. Violence.   I. Title.

RC569.5.V55R44   1997   616.85982   C97-930349-4

Key Porter Books Limited
70 The Esplanade
Toronto, Ontario
Canada M5E 1R2

Design: Peter Maher
Electronic Formatting: Heidi Palfrey
Printed and bound in Canada

97 98 99 00 6 5 4 3 2 1

To my wife, Barbara Lewis, whose alchemical powers turn darkness into light.

Contents

Acknowledgments

This book owes its life to my superb and wise editor, Charis Wahl; the strong and very patient support of Susan Renouf, editor-in-chief and president of Key Porter Books; and publisher Anna Porter's unflagging enthusiasm.

The determination to begin work on this book came on the heels of a television segment on violence that I co-produced several years ago with my friend and esteemed colleague Paul Slavin at ABC News. Over the years, and especially now in his senior producer role at ABC, Paul has helped make it possible for me to continue to enjoy being a producer at the network while I tend to my writing projects.

I also wish to thank my friend and colleague John McKenzie, a top-notch correspondent at ABC News. One of John's missions in life is to seek excellence in his work. His determination and success in this regard is highly inspiring. And John, thanks for being so forgiving during the writing of this book, when my darker moods would surface.

And thank you, Alan Morantz, friend and editor-in-chief at *Equinox* magazine, for encouraging my interest in writing about the brain. Some of the material on neuroscientist Michael Persinger in chapter four of this book first appeared in *Equinox*.

As the bibliography in this book indicates, there are numerous individuals to thank whose work is reflected in my arguments about violence and the brain. I would highly recommend these books and articles as a program of study to anyone willing to entertain basic questions about what it means to be human.

First Word

I call it the "look in the mirror" technique, a mode of self-evaluation that accompanies each morning's ritual of teeth brushing, face washing, hair combing and worried glances (from various angles) at what might be kindly considered an aging physique.

The mirror technique is simple, yet daring, as it involves staring into my own eyes and asking if I am looking at the person I really want to be.

The answer is usually a qualified yes. I often have looked into those eyes and wondered if my life might have been less stressful had I written about "safe" issues rather than topics that tend to be socially and/or politically volatile. I have, on occasion, wondered whether I might have been more content had I pursued a life relatively free from mental turmoil and intellectual conflict. No matter what I see in the mirror on any particular day, however, I believe that my sense of self, like yours, is the product of a powerful dialogue between brain and environment. I am a creature of evolution and culture, a being in constant creation. My mirrored image appears solid enough, but I sense that I can almost see the brain's energy taking in the new day, inundating me with competing ideas, some of which will seem to die, while others survive the processing.

This book on violence represents the complex process of giving life, however temporary and incomplete, to thoughts and emotions that have powerfully gripped me for many years. I found myself attracted to the subject of violence because it afforded the opportunity to delve deeply into the human condition, to investigate what informs that sense of self that we appraise in the mirror.

My goal here is not to overwhelm the reader with the highly detailed and voluminous research on the brain and violence, but rather, to focus on ideas. The tentative conclusions that I have reached about violence challenge the way we tend to see ourselves; they also challenge some of our fundamental beliefs, such as the notion of a mind and/or soul.

I see ideas as units of information that impinge upon brain cells and are capable of making a difference in how we behave. Thus, this book may make a difference in how we face up to violence.

The material presented here is divided into three parts. The first deals with our potential for violence. The second focuses on forms of violence, from the common to the extreme. The third examines controversial issues related to violence, such as media imagery, guns, prison and personal responsibility, and contemplates the future of violence.

Those seeking a quick fix for violence won't find it here; violence is not fixable. It is a staple of being human. Rather, this book endeavors to dispel common myths about violence and to challenge inept social policy that is fostering a totalitarian future.

Nicholas Regush
January 1997

1

OUR POTENTIAL

FOR VIOLENCE

1

The Changing Story
of the Mind:

How We Understand Violence

I

On February 12, 1993, in Liverpool, England, two ten-year-old boys
tortured and battered a two-year-old boy to death. The case made
headlines everywhere.

As one might expect, *society* saw to it that the murderers were
apprehended, and then punished, thereby reaffirming its moral
authority. Some of us probably cheered the boys' incarceration.

What exactly happened that day, the step-by-step progression
that led to murder, may never come to light; probably it is not even
fully remembered by the murderers. But there is much that is now rea-
sonably clear: Jon Venables and Robert Thompson lured James Bulger
from a shopping mall to a railroad track more than two miles away,
where they threw rocks at him and repeatedly brutalized him by
bashing his head with bricks. Finally, one of the boys cracked his skull
with a twenty-two-pound steel bar. They then left him to die on the
track, covered with bricks. Police found Bulger's body the next day,
cut in two by a train.

Because the shopping mall's security videotape showed images of
two children leading Bulger out of the mall, the police were able to
narrow their investigation. Paul Britton, a forensic psychologist,

advised detectives that the young suspects would likely be regular tru-
ants and street-wise. Both Venables and Thompson were under-
achievers in school, and petty thieves, and both lived in a poor
working-class neighborhood near the scene of the crime. They
appeared to fit the profile. And both had played hookey on the day
of Bulger's murder.

Police tapes of the early interrogations of the two boys reveal
they both denied taking part in the murder. But then Thompson
slipped up. Admitting that he had seen Bulger at the mall, he further
aroused police suspicions when he recalled that the two-year-old had
worn a blue coat. Under persistent questioning, both boys broke
down and confessed their crime.

The jury took less than six hours to reach a guilty verdict. The
court committed the boys to a juvenile center, where they will remain
until they become eighteen. The next stop will be a young offenders'
unit and, if judged one day to be "rehabilitated," they may go free.

Case closed? Not if we want to make some sense of violence.

As a get-tough public attitude toward crime and violence is common
in many industrialized societies, an expression of outrage might seem
an appropriate response to an unusually brutal murder—by children,
no less.

The Bulger case, however, can point us in a more revealing direction;
it can help us to broaden our understanding of violence. Particularly
striking was the tendency of both experts and the public to view
Venables and Thompson as somehow not quite human. Separating
"them" from "us" made it easy to label them "monsters," or "animals."
Angry mobs attacked the vans transporting Venables and Thompson to
trial. It sometimes appeared that only the police presence kept some of
the demonstrators from tearing Bulger's murderers to bits.

Media coverage of both the murder and the trial helped to demonize
Venables and Thompson. By focusing on what is generally perceived as
"the evil that walks among us," the headlines and images reaffirmed the
boundaries of society—what we will and will not tolerate. In so doing,

they emphasized the difference between *them* and *us*, serving the function once performed by public hangings.

The "otherness" of the boys was, for example, often described in terms of dark nature, or "evil," a religious concept that can be traced back to ancient times. After the trial, the judge was quoted widely as characterizing Bulger's murder as an act of "unparalleled evil and brutality." Detective Sergeant Philip Roberts of the Merseyside Police, a top cop on the case, proposed that "human nature from time to time produces freaks—in this case, evil freaks." He also referred to the crime as "evil torture." And evil not without deliberation: the boys were determined to kill, he said. These ten-year-olds set out to abduct a child, spotted Bulger, marched him away from the mall, decided to kill him and tried to make it look like a train accident. Forensic psychologist Paul Britton offered the opinion to the media that the boys killed Bulger because "they discovered they enjoyed the sadistic pleasure that comes from the pain."

Is violence as simple as that? The jury believed so, apparently.

Once Venables and Thompson confessed to murdering Bulger, there was likely little chance that they could avoid being held criminally responsible for the toddler's death. For the boys to escape conviction, it would have been necessary to show proof that they were *not* in control of their actions. The British legal system (the American and Canadian, as well) is heavily stacked against this line of defense, which often necessitates proving insanity or a diminished capacity to tell right from wrong. In short, the murderer's *mind* must somehow have lost control, either temporarily or chronically, and the act of murder has to have been involuntary and lacking in purpose.

When the psychiatrists who examined the boys reported to the court that there was no sign of an "abnormality of mind," the jury could not excuse the defendants from having committed murder; Venables and Thompson had willfully crossed the line to the Dark Side.

Some of us choose good, the explanation goes; and some of us, who have a darker nature, choose evil. Naturally the evil-doers must be held accountable and punished. The law must, on behalf of the good, institutionally isolate the bad from the rest of us, to free society of their wickedness. The social order is thereby strengthened. *We* are safe from *them*.

At this point in the argument, we are at the edge of very unpopular, yet challenging territory. You may want to play it safe and seek out a book that reiterates that violence is wrong and must be punished and that people generally are capable of controlling their violent urges, if only they try hard enough. And you may support politicians who insist that the best way to contain violence is by adding to the numbers of police patrolling our streets and by building more prisons, in order to control the evil behavior of those who refuse to control it themselves.

These views, passed on from one generation to the next, hinge on a widely held conception of the "mind"—a free-surfing, willful mind that can choose good or evil; an autonomous mind that makes right or wrong decisions; a mind that decides to kill or not kill, to harm or not harm.

This is a vision of the mind that this book will challenge.

Ask people at random what the "mind" is and you will get a casual variety of responses: The mind is the soul. The mind is the energy of the universe. The mind is in the head. The mind is independent of the brain, is connected to the brain, is the brain.

It is generally assumed that the mind operates like a central switchboard to govern behavior. That some central "I" casts and directs the show. That it is this "I" that confers our individuality, makes us who we are. Thus even children like Venables and Thompson can be judged in terms of willfulness of mind or evil purpose. Consequently, we can easily separate "them" from "us."

But what is the foundation of this notion? One need probe only gently to discover that the mind's story has been largely told in the language of philosophical reflection and speculation rather than of science. This notion we call "mind" didn't always exist. Relative to the span of human history, the concept of the mind is very new, indeed.

Before the mind as we know it, there was only spirit. According to historian Bruno Snell, writing in *The Discovery of the Mind*, the Greeks of the ninth century B.C. were unaware that they had thoughts and emotions. Human initiative was seen to be planned and executed by a spirit world. In Homer's *Iliad*, the gods send humans messages for daily living, for either their benefit or their destruction. There are no words for "consciousness" in this famous work, no indications of self-awareness in Homer's characters. There is no central, cohesive "I" that commands an individual's fate.

Other ancients also believed in a spirit world that determined life in a well-designed and ordered universe. Mesopotamian cuneiform texts contain numerous references to the commands of the spirit world, decreeing how to plant crops and on whom to wage war. The Old Testament records a similar belief system common among the ancient Hebrews.

It wasn't until about 600 B.C. that the mind as we know it began to be discovered. In India, the Buddha taught that human thoughts were the products of sensations and perceptions. In China, Confucius taught that each person was capable of decision.

In Greece, it had become evident that mere mortals could not attain the high moral standards attributed to the gods. This understanding gave rise to a more widespread focus on the individual, and it was the early Greek lyricists who began to explore the possibility that emotions arose from within rather than from celestial voices.

The search for self-knowledge and for understanding of the natural world followed. In the Greek city-states of the fifth and fourth centuries B.C., philosophical inquiry flourished, as did the pursuit of art and science. The Greeks voyaged inward in the hope of unraveling the great mysteries of human psychology. Their focus on divining the origins of thought set in motion questions about the mind that would preoccupy scholars up to the present day: Is the mind spirit or matter? Is mind connected to soul? Does mind exist after bodily death? Greek thinkers also anticipated the nature–nurture controversy, wondering whether the human condition results from inborn tendencies or from upbringing.

The Greeks, however, were limited in their reflection about the mind; they lacked the scientific tools to push beyond speculation. So were Roman scholars, who mostly tinkered with Greek ideas about the mind. And with the ascendancy of Christianity paralleling the demise of the Roman Empire, doctrine replaced free inquiry: the mind or soul was immaterial; after death, the soul left the body to become immortal.

This vision of human nature became entrenched in Christian writings that carved out and dominated Western European thinking throughout the feudal period. Often referred to as the "Dark Ages," it was a time of fiefdoms, long battles, holy wars, the Black Death and intellectual stagnation.

It wasn't until the invention of printing in the mid-fifteenth century that study became feasible outside Church-controlled universities. The printed word, along with the greater contact with other cultures, led to the rediscovery of philosophical investigation and the sustained development of a science of the mind. Church teachings gradually came to be cast in a more secular context. Nowhere did this fine-tuning occur more dramatically and in a more enduring form than in the seventeenth-century works of Renaissance philosopher and physicist René Descartes. The mind, he wrote, was a spiritual substance that gave rise to our ability to be certain of our very existence. The mind was the part of us that thinks. Hence, his famous dictum, "I think, therefore I am" (*Cogito ergo sum*).

Descartes embraced advances in physics that portrayed the universe as a massive machine. (God was the clockmaker who had wound up the world.) Whereas the mind was accessible only through rational reflection, the human body, as a part of the mechanism of the universe, should be explored scientifically. Discoveries about the body could shed light on the cosmos. Thus, Descartes renewed the split of mind from body.

He was, of course, dead wrong in postulating that the seat of interaction between mind and brain was the pineal gland, a tiny cone-shaped structure deep within the skull. But all the same, Descartes's theory has had extraordinary staying power. Even the modern flood of knowledge about the brain has yet to dislodge the popular notion of immaterial mind as the be-all of human consciousness. The concept of the mind in Western institutions—including the notion of personal responsibility that is at the heart of judicial proceedings—remains heavily influenced by, if not locked into, a fundamentally medieval theology.

Since Descartes, philosophers and scientists have issued strong challenges to mind–body dualism; indeed, much of our development of a psychology of mind can be viewed as an effort to knock off Descartes. Even his philosophical contemporaries in England, whose search for knowledge was grounded in experiment or observation rather than in theory, argued that mind must be a by-product of brain processes. Thomas Hobbes, a major force in empiricism, referred to any talk about the soul as an exercise in vanity, if not gibberish. David Hume didn't feel that the nature of the soul was worthy of discussion. These empiricists instead contended that the mind arose from sense experience. How this could be so and what it suggested about the ability to make willful choices and decisions remain the focus of much scientific attention.

The scientific approach to behavior has its roots in the work of early anatomists. By the year 200 B.C., much of the structure of the nervous system, visible to the eye, had been mapped. Back then, however, only relatively primitive theories were proposed about how the body's sensory system operated. The Greek anatomist Galen held that movement occurred when nerves, transporting a vital spirit, puffed up muscles. (Descartes, many centuries later, still ventured that muscles moved because they were infused with "animal spirits.") Variations of "vitalism" held on until the nineteenth century, when an experimental approach to the nervous system began to produce a more material concept of behavior.

This new era ushered in a mix of pseudoscience and seminal brain research. Skull reading, or phrenology—the practice of associating bumps on the head with personality traits—became a fashionable entertainment, while scientists found that specific behavior could be associated with specific regions of the brain. The left side of the brain, for instance, became known as the center of language function and self-awareness, the right side as controlling visual and spatial tasks. Anatomic studies began to reveal the physical connections of one brain part to another.

Such scientific psychology gave support to a parallel assault on vitalism, Charles Darwin's theory of evolution. In 1859, Darwin published *On the Origin of Species*, in which he adjusted and rephrased earlier ideas—that life and the universe were the products of slow change—and established his own vision based on a principle he termed "natural selection." This was a shaping process whereby the genetic characteristics that offered organisms the best chance to reproduce were carried over to the next generation. In *The Descent of Man*, published in 1871, Darwin offered evidence to suggest that humans had evolved from animals.

Natural selection, a mechanistic concept, was the antithesis of a God-designed universe. As philosopher Daniel Dennett writes in *Darwin's Dangerous Idea*, "Before Darwin, order and design came down from God. The whole universe was his artifact. A product of his intelligence. His mind." In Darwin's world-view, God and a non-material mind were unnecessary to the unfolding of life and human behavior. Natural selection did the design work, including that of developing the elaborate neural processes of the brain, processes which give us our thoughts, goals and emotions. Darwin had thus planted the seed of a new psychology—one that focused on the mind as a common human product deeply rooted in the biology of the species as well as in the ongoing idiosyncrasies of everyday cultural forces. The nature of the interaction between biology and environment would be the subject of much debate and controversy.

But, by the end of the nineteenth century, an increasingly deterministic psychology dismissed mind as mere superstition and largely abandoned the goal of understanding the brain's machinery as it applied to human behavior. Why bother, if human beings were essentially stimulus–response units, conditioned by the external world? There was certainly no room for concepts such as free will and personal responsibility. By the 1920s, "behaviorism," as it came to be known, dominated psychology and resulted in proposals whereby human behavior could be engineered by means of positive reinforcement. B.F. Skinner, a leading behaviorist, envisioned that conditioning techniques could be used to program an entire community to live in peace and harmony. He named his fictional world "Walden II."

But even at the height of its acceptance, behaviorism was considered extreme. Certainly it was deemed necessary to cleanse the study of human behavior of unnecessary religious debris, such as the concept of a non-material mind; however, behaviorism's insistence that humans learned solely via positive reinforcement, much like caged pigeons conditioned to peck at a lever to release a food pellet, seemed too simple.

Surely humans are more complicated than that? Humans have memory. They have personality. They reason. They create. They solve problems. They make moral decisions. Some psychologists found the mental processes underlying these human attributes to be worthy of study. As a result, psychology was to look inward again, but this time without any reliance on gods or spirit.

In the past several decades, a confluence of efforts to study how the brain produces what has long been called "mind" has resulted in a broad body of experimentation, involving brain imaging, molecular biology and genetics, often referred to as "neuroscience."

Neuroscience has located no place in the brain where all the information necessary to produce experience or consciousness comes together. Rather, the brain appears to work in networks or modules. At any given moment, sensory cells from, say, the eye, ear, nose and skin shuttle environmental information along cranial nerves to specific regions of the brain's cerebral cortex. Different parts of the brain analyze incoming shapes, textures, sounds, smells and colors. These units of information are then somehow bound together, and we experience our surroundings. How this may occur has been proposed by Sir Francis Crick, of the Salk Institute, and by Christoff Koch, of the California Institute of Technology. They suggest that the unity of experience arises from the synchronized firings of basic brain cells, called "neurons," which bind information routed and processed in different parts of the brain.

One implication of this premise is that there is no mind separate from the brain. No "ghost" in the "machine" that is our body. No shadings of the soul to account for behavior. Only billions of nerve cells with trillions of connections, processing sensory data, with the help of brain chemicals, to produce consciousness.

More directly put: Our sense of self is constructed *moment to moment* by a vast array of neurons and the message-carrying chemicals they produce. Therefore, change the configuration of the brain's neuro-chemistry and you change the sense of who you are and of your place in the world.

In this light, we must also consider whether changes in, or damage to, the brain may alter consciousness, and therefore behavior. Malnourishment, tumors, beatings, infections, drug and alcohol use, seizures, hormonal defects and/or heavy-metals contamination are some of the factors that affect the brain's chemical configuration. The chem-ical messengers, or "neurotransmitters," that these factors affect perform a vital function in the production of consciousness: they decode and encode sensory data, relaying them from one brain cell to another.

"Mechanistic reduction," as it is usually tagged, reduces us—and the mind—to the functioning of neurons. It also runs counter to the cherished dualistic belief that our essence as individuals is somehow greater than the body and that it outlives the body. For this reduc-tionism accepts the inevitability of the annihilation of the self: when the brain dies, the self also dies.

Patricia Churchland, a philosopher at the Salk Institute and University of San Diego, suggests in *Neurophilosophy* that even those who intellectually are materialists have a tough time emotionally accepting this conclusion: "They have a negative gut reaction to the idea that neurons—cells that you can see under a microscope and probe with electrodes, brains you can hold in one hand and that rapidly rot without oxygen supply—are the source of subjectivity and the 'me-ness' of me . . . An explanation of something as special as what makes me me should really involve, the feeling is, something more deep and mysterious and other-worldly than mere neurons."

As one might therefore expect, not all neuroscientists emphasize the hard reductionism that explains emotion, thoughts and behavior solely in terms of the brain's remarkable computational powers. Some neuroscientists, including Gerald Edelman of the Scripps Research Institute, offer a softer picture, arguing the brain is not a computer but a densely interconnected and changing tapestry of neurons that routinely copes with and integrates new information coming from the environment. The brain, he theorizes, works according to the laws of evolution, constantly adapting to changing circumstances. The precise structure of each person's brain will therefore be different; the networks of neural connections begin to establish themselves as a unique but flexible signature during early stages of development. Consciousness results from the steady integration into the brain of the ongoing impact of millions of these neuron connections in response to changing environmental conditions.

Neuroscience is certainly young enough to entertain a wide range of theories about the nature of consciousness for many years to come. The overriding fact remains, however, that a scientific view of human psychology is still not incorporated into our daily life and institutions. We have not even begun to grapple with how a more material view of mind might affect our sense of self, and of that self in relation to others. On the societal level, we are still functioning as dualists.

This is very much the way we view the violence in our midst. It is non-threatening to believe in a discrete mind that serves a policing function, rooting out the bad from the good. We would still prefer to accept the existence of a mind that can choose right or wrong, rather than to profoundly change the way we think about ourselves. We also find it convenient to categorize humans as violent or non-violent, and to separate the violent from the rest of society. We believe that quarantining the likes of young Robert Thompson and Jon Venables can prevent their darkness from contaminating others.

However, if we paid more attention to understanding violence as a product of brain processes, we might better appreciate how malleable consciousness is. The elements of the brain that produce consciousness can be as vulnerable as a knee joint. Under the right biological and social conditions, the brain may well unleash aggression ranging from a simple threat to extreme savagery. If we can acknowledge this, we might be willing to face up to the likelihood that every human has the potential to harm or kill. We might no longer be quite so willing to divide the world into "them" and "us."

II

Since the eighteenth century, violence has most often been considered to be the opposite of reason. It was widely postulated then—as it often is now—that society can be free of violence, that we can live in a truly civilized society, if only we have the will to do so and put our minds to it. In fact, we like to think that we have already moved from barbarism to rationality. Violence is therefore typically assumed to come from "outside." Violence visits us.

All around us, every day, we can see examples of cooperation, kindness and gentleness. It can't be stated emphatically enough that we live in a world in which mutual aid is very common.

But there's also the nastier side of life, as offered up regularly in newspaper headlines and TV broadcasts, which often reinforce the "otherness" of violence. The media tend to focus on the most vicious assaults, often providing explicit, gory details: How eight middle-class high-school athletes in New Jersey used a broom handle, baseball bat and dirty stick to assault a seventeen-year-old girl with a mental age of eight; how, in Houston, six members of the gang Black N White raped two girls, and then strangled them to death; how a New York City teen drove a steel-reinforced boot through the lens of a man's glasses, leaving him in a pool of blood on the subway; and how, in San Francisco, a gunman with three semi-automatic pistols entered the office of a legal firm and opened fire on a glassed-in conference room, killing eight people and wounding six others before shooting himself.

Stories such as these, because they involve youth or what appears to be particularly thoughtless violence, become media events and color public awareness and discussion of life's dark side. The media gave the Bulger murder a high profile because it involved children and seemed to be especially brutal. Most acts of murder and everyday violence, however, never make the newspapers or television news. The vast majority of assaults are suffered without public acknowledgment, often in silence. Usually there is little or no recourse.

In the United States, for example, an extremely violent society compared with most others, there are usually about 25,000 homicides and more than 1.5 million assaults reported annually. About 130,000 rapes are put on record, although a credible estimate of the actual number of rapes is at least 500,000. And each year, between 2 and 4 million women suffer physical abuse, including 8 to 11 percent of all pregnant American women. Nor is the workplace a safe haven: annually about 110,000 violent incidents in U.S. workplaces are reported.

Relatively few of these cases of violence make headlines. The same is true of the estimated 2 to 4 million children who suffer abuse or neglect, and the estimated 1 million elders who are mistreated, by their families or in institutions.

The occasional survey focusing on violent behavior suggests that the scope and amount of "hidden" violence may be considerable. For example, the findings of a phone survey released in November 1993 by the Canadian government, perhaps the first of its kind in the world, focused on a random sample of 12,300 women:

Fifty percent had experienced sexual or physical violence at least once since age sixteen; one woman in ten experienced violence within the year prior to the survey. Of those who had been or are married, 29 percent said their current or previous partner had physically abused them. Twenty-five percent of the women were either pushed or grabbed; 25 percent were threatened; 19 percent were slapped; 15 percent had had something thrown at them; 11 percent were kicked, bitten or hit; 9 percent were beaten; 8 percent were sexually assaulted; 7 percent were battered with an object; and 5 percent were shot or knifed.

The survey also revealed that, of the women who said they had been assaulted, 22 percent had never told anyone about the incident.

When violence is brought into the light, it becomes clear that it is not "out there," or separate from us: violence is us.

When we look closely at the violent villains in the high-profile shockers of the day, we see that horrific violent acts are not necessarily committed by people who appear to be monsters.

After a mass murderer or serial killer is apprehended, neighbors interviewed by the press are often surprised: "He was such a nice man, very quiet" or, "Looking at him, you'd never think he could hurt anyone."

A sociologist might refer to the belief that killers should look different from "us" as "Lombrosian." In 1876, Cesare Lombroso, the Italian crime specialist, wrote *L'uomo delinquente* (translated into English in 1911), in which he argued that the "born criminal" could be identified by his "physical stigmata"—such characteristics as lobeless ears, receding chin and crooked nose.

We may have cast Lombroso's data aside as academically weak, if not silly, but we nonetheless seem to nurture his self-serving illusion. For, by whatever means, society has always distinguished between "them," the evil-doers, and "us," the good people. Yet the line of separation is crossed more easily than we like to admit, as shown by a classic study published in 1963.

Psychologist Stanley Milgram was interested in the relationship of aggression and obedience in the aftermath of the Holocaust. Like other social scientists, he was perplexed by the savagery shown toward other human beings during wartime by so-called normal German individuals. At Yale, he selected forty male subjects, aged twenty to fifty, from a cross-section of the population and convinced them to participate in a study that would focus on memory and learning.

These subjects were asked to think of themselves as teachers. Milgram instructed them to inflict higher and higher levels of electric shock on a "student" when he incorrectly performed a word skill. The student was, of course, Milgram's accomplice in the study, as was the "researcher" in the white lab coat supervising the test. The shock generator was, of course, fake. Milgram actually wanted to see if his subjects would become sadists.

The results were provocative. Milgram reported that most of the "teachers" reacted negatively to the task, even showing signs of stress, but nonetheless obeyed the researcher's commands to continue to inflict pain, even when they heard screams from the accomplice, who had informed the teachers that he had a heart condition. An amazed

Milgram wrote: "In a large number of cases, the degree of tension reached extremes that are rarely seen in sociopsychological laboratory studies. Subjects were observed to sweat, tremble, bite their lips, groan, and dig their fingernails into their flesh . . . A mature and initially poised businessman enter[ed] the laboratory smiling and confident. Within 20 minutes, he was reduced to a twitching, stuttering wreck who was rapidly approaching a point of nervous collapse . . . yet he continued to respond to every word of the experimenter, and obeyed to the end." Milgram concluded that his subjects became obedient in the name of science, adding that, in a society that teaches children to obey authority unquestioningly, such extreme behavior might be expected.

Although Milgram's study has been replicated in several countries, the laboratory conclusions cannot—and should not—be extrapolated unreservedly to "real life" situations. The study, however, demonstrated that ordinary people under strong pressure will obey orders that might be reprehensible to them under "normal" conditions. Indeed, it appears that anyone may be capable of inflicting pain, or of killing.

In *Eichmann in Jerusalem*, political historian Hannah Arendt, writing of the Jerusalem trial of Nazi Adolf Eichmann, concludes that "the trouble with Eichmann was precisely that so many were like him, and that the many were neither perverted, nor sadistic, that they were, and still are, terribly and terrifyingly normal."

Were the American soldiers who went on a well-documented three-hour killing orgy in My Lai, Vietnam, perverted or sadistic, or were they, too, revealing their human potential for violence? On March 16, 1968, a platoon of U.S. soldiers, under the command of Lieutenant William Laws Calley, Jr., slaughtered about 500 unarmed civilian women, children and elders, raping some of the women before killing them. Many of the soldiers even joked as they threw grenades at the innocents. According to accounts gathered by Subnev Babuta and Jean-Claude Bragard in their book *Evil*, the men later understood that the horrors of war had led them to perceive their victims as 'things,' not as human beings.

Perhaps pivotal in this case of wartime savagery is the fact that Calley's initial order to kill was ignored. Only when he returned to the scene and himself started shooting did his troops go berserk. Authority ruled the day.

Students of military training know that such a display of desensitization is the result of fairly common indoctrination. U.S. lieutenant-colonel Dave Grossman states in *On Killing*, his analysis of killing patterns in the military, that conditioning techniques to overcome a common resistance to killing have become increasingly sophisticated. The programming aims to develop quick firing behavior in a soldier. Grossman points out that authority and group pressure and feelings of being distant (either culturally or morally) from the enemy eventually overcome strong resistance to killing.

This is not a theory. The military banks on the fact that anyone can kill.

III

It is not easy to face up to the idea that violence, much like cooperation, is a staple of being human. That excessive amounts of violence can be triggered in *anyone*. That we must learn to live with violence, and, one hopes, in the process come to better understand it, and perhaps even tame some of its excesses.

Instead, however, our culture reinforces an old—and fanciful—view of the mind that endows it with the power to control the inner beast, at will: those of us who have this self-control will not become violent; those who lose control will cause murder and mayhem—them and us.

Modern brain science suggests that this distinction is a myth. One theory is that we all lack this policing function of the mind over the brain because the mind does not exist independent of the brain. The mind is a brain product. Violence, according to this concept of the mind, may be merely a bunch of firing neurons.

There are powerful forces, both in the human brain and in society, that serve to facilitate violence, and other processes that serve to inhibit violence. This book will reveal how this delicate balance can be disturbed, sometimes quite easily. It can be disturbed in people who rape, murder, desecrate human bodies. It can be disturbed in people who attack and injure their spouses, their children, their parents, their friends, their co-workers. And it can be disturbed by sudden, explosive insults to the brain as well as by slow, chronic injury or subtle changes, short- or long-term.

Seen in this light, violence is not a behavioral aberration, but a basic human potentiality that we may have no control over, or will often draw upon in everyday life to resolve our needs and conflicts—at home, on the job, on the streets. Though we live cooperatively with others, we also live in a world rife with inequalities, corruption and discord, and one which provokes rivalry, greed, frustration and hatred. Why should it be so surprising that violent expression is a part of so much that we do? Why should it be so surprising that our lives often are driven by conflict and various forms of violence?

To reduce violence significantly, both in its high-profile excesses and its day-to-day hidden forms, would require extraordinary shifts in our learning and belief systems; major changes in our everyday environments, many of which facilitate violence; and considerable alteration of the flow of information into the brain. It would require a world with little conflict, and a brain with little potential for directing violence. This is obviously not going to happen. It is not likely that we will see violence diminish in our lifetime. If anything, we should expect it to escalate worldwide as social structures come under heavy assault from the hungry, the disenfranchised and the embittered. And in a world of environmental degradation and rapid technological change, we can also expect increasing numbers of individuals to be pushed to the breaking point.

Meanwhile, our responses to violence—our laws, our justice systems, our social and political institutions—remain far out of line with the realities of violence. They are geared to a world-view of "them" and "us," a view that nurtures totalitarian thinking and propels society toward strong-arm social control and a heightening of social conflict. As Leonard Cohen wrote, "I see the future, brother. It is murder."

2

Battlelines:

The Controversy over Research into Violence

I

For many decades, science has attempted to make sense of violence: to determine why it occurs and who may be particularly predisposed to causing others harm. The answers have not come easily. Even raising the questions has created social unease and provoked hostility. To probe the nature of violence has required forays into areas of deep controversy, including the mind–brain debate and the age-old argument about the relative contributions to human behavior of genetic heritage versus culture. These issues are often colored by religious convictions and political agendas. Add a dash of scientific insensitivity, bravado, ineptitude and racism, and you end up with a recipe for social conflict.

Take the events that track back to February 11, 1992, in Bethesda, Maryland. It all started with unthinking words, and escalated over several months into a fiery battle about the right to conduct research focused on possible links between violence and biological factors such as brain processes and genes, our hereditary materials. On that day, speaking at a public meeting, Frederick Goodwin, an influential psychiatrist, author of more than a hundred scholarly papers, and the head of the federal government's Drug Abuse and Mental Health

Administration, presented some ideas about violence, but unintentionally did so in language that triggered widespread outrage. He theorized that deep-seated biological urges can be unleashed if social controls are removed. He then suggested that perhaps in certain "high-impact inner-city areas," which he equated with "jungles," males behave like hyperaggressive and hypersexual monkeys.

Had Goodwin planned to be inflammatory, he could not have done much better. In a letter to the *Wall Street Journal*, Michigan politician John Conyers, one of many people who jumped on Goodwin's comments, described them as "dangerous," and accused him of perpetuating the idea that blacks are defective. Goodwin was, Conyers claimed, creating a "smokescreen for the separate and discriminatory treatment of African Americans."

Louis Sullivan, the black physician who then headed the U.S. Department of Health and Human Services, reprimanded Goodwin for being "offensive and insensitive." Goodwin apologized.

The United States is consistently the most violent peacetime nation on earth. The 1992 statistics, as usual, were harrowing: more than 6 million violent crimes were committed, including 25,000 murders. In response to what he perceived to be an ongoing epidemic of violence, Sullivan had been preparing the coordination of a government-sponsored effort to address the issue.

The statistics underscored the disadvantage of being black in the United States. Blacks make up about 12 percent of the population but were arrested for about 45 percent of the violent crimes; 1 in 27 black men died violently, compared with 1 in 205 white men; 1 in 117 black women died violently, compared with 1 in 496 white women. Blacks appeared to be living in a deeply entrenched cycle of tragedy.

Sullivan believed that one way out of this predicament would be a solid research effort to develop effective measures for preventing violence. The government's statistics showed that most violent youth offenses were committed by about 7 percent of the youth population; Sullivan hoped that well-targeted risk-intervention programs could eventually reduce violence, first among youth, and gradually throughout the inner cities.

Sullivan's plan called for research on the loss of employment, poverty, absence of role models, drug abuse and community-outreach programs. As well, biological studies would explore how genes and brain processes might contribute to the likelihood of violence.

At the time, there was already federally funded research under way on ways to predict violence. Some studies were examining how changing amounts of certain brain chemicals might be associated with violence. Most of the studies, however, were attempting to isolate psychological and environmental factors that might identify youths likely to commit violent acts. In all, about $40 million in federal money was being spent on violence research. Sullivan's plan would boost the total to about $50 million, still relatively modest funding. (The U.S. government spends about $1.4 billion on AIDS research annually.)

Sullivan's call-to-arms against violence also made sense in the light of the latest developments in brain science. Study of brain chemicals was showing how their supplies were associated with shifts in behavior and feelings. And some of these types of brain changes were even being captured on film by powerful technologies, known as "magnetic resonance imaging" and "positron emission tomography." Studies of specific brain chemicals, particularly serotonin, thought to be associated with violence were suggesting that environmental pressures, such as living in the tough inner city, could dramatically alter a person's potential for aggressive behavior. On the basis of these new theories and preliminary findings, it was reasonable for Sullivan to view contemporary brain science as at least one pathway to a better understanding of violence and, possibly, a better way to control it.

Sullivan, however, naively dubbed his plan the "Violence Initiative," not taking into account how this phrase might be interpreted by those with concerns about major government offensives to correct social behavior. Nor could he have anticipated how his employee, Goodwin, would fan the flames.

On May 5, Goodwin was reassigned (and, technically, demoted) by Sullivan to head the National Institute of Mental Health (NIMH). In his address to the annual meeting of the American Psychiatric Association, he steered clear of equating inner-city males with monkeys, but made the

Violence Initiative a bigger target for critics by unveiling more details.

Goodwin called his speech "Conduct Disorder as a Precursor to Adult Violence and Substance Abuse: Can the Progression Be Halted?" In it, he referred to the escalation of violence in American society during the past thirty years and suggested, as he had on February 11, that the "societal glues" that keep life civil are becoming ineffectual. He offered the examples of epidemic drug abuse, increasing use of alcohol, the rejection of children by their parents and the deterioration of inner cities. Even so, he advised, only relatively few of the individuals living in fragile environments become violent criminals. Might it be possible to identify these individuals early, before they meet up with the prison system? The idea behind the initiative would be "to figure out which of the children really need help." Goodwin estimated that perhaps as many as 15 percent of schoolchildren could eventually be tagged by their teachers as vulnerable and given support, including counseling and skills training, and even medical care, if necessary.

To accomplish this goal, attention had to be given to biological factors such as head injuries resulting from physical abuse, brain chemistry and low IQ. However, Goodwin emphasized, experimental ways must also be found to study the interaction of psychosocial and biological forces.

Goodwin concluded that the role of genetic influences in conduct disorders "is currently ill-defined," but allowed that some genetic component, "not by any means overwhelming," could be involved in antisocial personality and criminality.

His more disciplined May 5 speech hardly shows him to be hell-bent on some devious, racist plan for the state control of undesirables; however, some government watchers viewed it as biological meddling in the lives of the poor and disenfranchised. Goodwin's speech simply did not strike a balance between the influence of biological triggers, such as changes in brain chemistry, and that of social factors, such as poverty, malnourishment, lack of jobs, and racism, which can also unleash violence. He appeared to be too preoccupied with the brain.

The most vociferous critic of the Violence Initiative was Peter Breggin, a psychiatrist in Bethesda, Maryland. He is the director of the

Center for the Study of Psychiatry, a non-profit network of about seventy-five individuals, including psychiatrists, lawyers, patients'-rights advocates and members of Congress.

Since its founding in 1971, the center, which doubles as Breggin's home, had been devoted to the reform of psychiatry. He had spoken out against such common practices as the use of brain-changing medications for mental illness, electroconvulsive therapy (electric "shock therapy") as a treatment for severe depression, and psychosurgery (treating mental illness by cutting nerve fibers in specific brain regions).

In the late 1960s and early 1970s, in the wake of ghetto riots, Breggin had fought successfully on behalf of a coalition of individuals and groups to stop federal funding of biological studies of violent behavior. He had charged that the federal strategy was to blame the rioters for social ills by finding criteria under which they could be judged to be genetically and biologically unfit.

Breggin reacted with outrage to Goodwin's speech. In a bulletin issued by the center, he wrote: "This biomedical approach directly threatens civil liberties, oppresses black children and their families, masks racist intentions, and distracts the nation from the true sources of pain, suffering and violence within the inner city." Breggin appears to believe that the only moral action is social action—countering racism, poverty and the deterioration of the inner city; to assess people's bodies and brains for error while they are living under such adverse conditions is immoral.

According to Breggin, the Violence Initiative would favor pharmaceuticals that dull violent tendencies over social programs to alleviate poverty and hunger and to provide jobs. In press releases from the center and in other publications, including a letter to the *New York Times*, he railed against the Violence Initiative.

As a concession to Breggin and fellow critics, the government established a scientific panel to review all the research into violence that federal agencies fund and to provide guidelines on how the research ought to be presented to the public.

A related controversy deals specifically with the relation between genes and violence, and how progress in this area of science is interpreted. Though there have been some intriguing advances that should be seen as worthy of strong consideration in any effort to better understand violence, such studies are preliminary, and often presented with too much enthusiasm and expectation.

One brouhaha resulted from plans to hold a conference on October 9, 1992, at the University of Maryland, entitled "Genetic Factors in Crime: Findings, Uses and Implications." The university's Institute for Philosophy and Public Policy, and the National Institutes of Health (NIH), the umbrella administration for all U.S. government science and research funding, were the sponsors. The plan was to address a wide range of concerns about genetics research in both completed and ongoing studies. Advocates of biological research were invited, as were critics.

It was the brochure advertising the conference that caused the row. One section was especially provocative:

> Researchers have already begun to study the genetic regulation of
> violent and impulsive behavior and to search for genetic markers
> associated with criminal conduct. Their work is motivated in part
> by the early success of research on the genetics of behavioral and
> psychiatric conditions like alcoholism and schizophrenia. But
> genetic research also gains impetus from the apparent failure of
> environmental approaches to crime-deterrence, diversion and
> rehabilitation—to affect the dramatic increases in crime, especially
> violent crime, that this country has experienced over the past 30
> years. Genetic research holds out the prospect of identifying
> individuals who may be predisposed to certain kinds of criminal
> conduct, of isolating environmental features which trigger those
> predispositions and of treating some predispositions with drugs and
> unintrusive therapies.

The brochure was mailed to about 10,000 potential participants just as Peter Breggin and some black leaders and academics were getting up in arms over Goodwin's Violence Initiative. Breggin and his coalition condemned the conference as pernicious propaganda; as further evidence that, in funding the conference, the federal government was intent on finding ways to interfere with daily life in the inner cities, probably by using prescription drugs, particularly with children, to quell signs of restlessness and non-compliance with authority.

One thing was certainly clear: the brochure's enthusiasm was more hype than science. Though there has been slow progress in linking single genes to certain diseases, it is quite another matter to claim a linkage between a single gene and complex behavior. Editorials in major journals, such as *Nature Genetics*, that focus on genetic research have warned scientists not to jump the gun.

Critics of the conference had reason to be contemptuous of the brochure, as there have been numerous displays of premature jubilation among behavioral geneticists. Here are some examples: In 1987, two scientific teams claimed to have located different genes linked to manic depression, one in Amish families and the other in Israeli families. The study results were later retracted. In 1988, a research group claimed to have identified a gene linked to schizophrenia in British and Icelandic families. This finding, too, proved groundless and was withdrawn. And, in 1990, a research group suggested it had linked a gene with alcoholism, but this has not panned out either.

In the summer of 1993, researchers at the National Cancer Institute in Bethesda, Maryland, claimed in *Science* that they were closing in on a "gay gene." The group, led by molecular biologist Dean Hamer, located in thirty-three of forty pairs of gay brothers an area of gene similarity at the end of the X chromosome, the only one that men inherit from their mother. Hamer predicted that a test for homosexuality was imminent. This idea received wide circulation in the media. The study, however, showed that the genetic pattern was not present in seven pairs of gay men, implying that more goes to the making of a homosexual than can be explained by a "gay gene."

There were several responses to this study. Some researchers quarreled with the results, saying Hamer ignored a constellation of environmental factors, such as personal experience, upbringing and family background, as contributing to sexual orientation. (It is worth mentioning that there has not been any independent replication of Hamer's data.)

However, Hamer's latest study, published in October 1995 in *Nature Genetics*, shows new evidence that genetic material on one segment of the X chromosome seems to influence the probability of homosexuality in males—though not in females. A larger study is in the planning stages.

What all this boils down to is that, while genes may well play a role in determining sexual orientation, it's very unlikely that there is anything as simple as a "gay gene." Or, for that matter, an alcoholism gene, a schizophrenia gene or a violence gene.

Even if a single gene did play an important role in some form of behavior, it is a considerable feat to track down one particular gene on a chromosome: each chromosome may contain several thousand genes; normal human cells contain twenty-three pairs of chromosomes. Such behavioral studies must also separate the genetic component from the environmental, and while researchers interested in criminal behavior and violence have made some progress, the results hardly qualify as heralding a new age in behavioral genetics.

The most widely cited genetics crime research was conducted in Denmark more than a decade ago by Sarnoff Mednick, a psychologist at the University of Southern California. Published in the journal *Science* in 1983, the study compared the criminal records of 14,427 men adopted by non-relatives in Denmark between 1927 and 1947 with the conviction records of their biological parents. (For the most part, the men were adopted by people with no criminal convictions.)

Mednick found that men who committed violent crimes tended to have a biological mother who had a mental illness and a biological father who committed property crimes. He also found that men who had many convictions for theft were likely to have biological fathers who also had theft convictions.

What did this study and similar findings in a study of adoptees in Sweden imply? Possibly that genes exert some influence on behavior, as the biological fathers and sons had half their genes in common. However, such studies stretch the available science to conclude that a gene will set off a predictable progression that causes the development of complex behavior. In fact, of course, social, economic and other factors are likely to be involved.

Another danger area is correlational studies, particularly as they typically involve small numbers of test subjects. A textbook example of what not to do in scientific research is found in correlational studies of criminality undertaken in the 1960s. The research linked criminal and aggressive behavior in a small group of men to the presence of an extra Y chromosome—that is, the men had forty-seven chromosomes instead of the usual forty-six. (This happens when a sperm with two Y chromosomes fuses with an egg. Men normally have one X and one Y chromosome. Women have two X chromosomes.)

The most thorough study focused on a group of men incarcerated in a high-security mental hospital in Scotland. It was reported that this prison population contained about twenty times the proportion of men with the extra Y chromosome than there was in the general population.

The researchers also characterized the men with the extra Y as unusually tall and mentally retarded. Thus, retardation, tallness and aggression were declared to be related to the extra Y. Subsequent prison studies and studies of the general population, however, showed that the vast majority of males with an extra Y are not unusually aggressive.

When scientific passions outrun verified fact, individuals are put at risk. On the basis of the early studies focusing on men with the extra Y chromosome, two Boston scientists thought they had a bright idea. They initiated a study to screen all boys born at an area hospital for the extra Y chromosome. The grand plan was to monitor these boys for many years at school, and at home, to detect "abnormalities," and to counsel families.

This ill-advised research died in the early 1970s, when scientific reason prevailed; however, gene-science research has been continuing, to determine how heredity may contribute to crime and violence. And there has been some progress in identifying defects in genes that might affect brain chemicals and, in turn, possibly contribute to a violent predisposition.

One study, published in October 1993 in *Science*, has received a lot of attention. It was conducted after a Dutch teacher tracing his family history began to wonder why so many of the males in his family were brawlers. He asked a group of scientists led by geneticist Han

Brunner at the University Hospital in Nijmegen, 60 miles east of Rotterdam, to determine whether this trait could be inherited.

Urine tests showed that five male family members, aged twenty to fifty, who were impulsively violent, abnormally metabolized an enzyme in the brain known as "MAOA" (monoamine oxidase A). The enzyme breaks down serotonin, among other brain chemicals. A lowering of the serotonin supply in the brain has been linked to violence. An examination of genes showed that all five men were deficient in a gene that produces MAOA. Twelve male family members who were not considered impulsively violent did not have the gene defect.

This finding is intriguing, but raises some questions: Is there sufficient information to brand the five men impulsively violent? Can this effect, if real, be demonstrated in a much wider population? These questions beg for further research.

A study published in *Science* in June 1995 showed that a MAOA-deficient strain of mice—that is, mice lacking the gene for the MAOA enzyme—exhibited aggression. Researchers were able to reverse the behavior by injecting the mice with a drug that duplicates MAOA's activity. Is there a possible therapy for at least that subset of individuals who become violent because of the same enzyme deficiency?

On a related front, a study published in November 1995 in *Nature* shows that male mice lacking a particular gene are oversexed and vicious. They were bred to lack a gene essential for the production of nitric oxide, which allows nerve cells to communicate. The researchers suggest that nitric oxide may normally serve as a brake on excessive and potentially dangerous behaviors, and that a lack of the chemical leads to wild, impulsive activity. Does this study hold out the possibility that some violence in humans may be similarly explained? Yes, of course. (The researchers, however, may have pushed the point a little too hard in their conclusions, and they received criticism for doing so.)

Thus, even today, the University of Maryland would have been hard pressed to highlight genetic research that lived up to the hype in the brochure used to promote its 1992 conference on genetics and crime. To the university's credit, in light of the ensuing criticism it admitted that the brochure had overstated the research advances in genetics, and offered to reprint the brochure with the necessary changes. Certainly, there had been inadequate scrutiny of the conference advertising on the university's part, but it was hardly a conspiracy to foster an unrealistic picture of scientific breakthroughs.

Nonetheless, Breggin's coalition was determined to kill the conference. The NIH, which had given the conference proposal a very positive review, withdrew $78,000 it had promised the conference organizers. The agency said that statements associated with the event, including those in the brochure, "inflamed public opinion"—the conference would have been an affront to the black community.

It certainly was an affront to those who had hoped to discuss openly the aspirations and pitfalls of gene science. The university appealed what was clearly a political rather than a scientific decision and won back their funding. The NIH appeals board also ruled that the agency had been unreasonable in not working with the university to revise the brochure. The board directed the agency to collaborate with the university in the planning of a rescheduled conference, which got off the ground in September 1995 under a new name: "The Meaning and Significance of Research on Genetics and Criminal Behavior." The revised title rightly conveyed greater neutrality. There was a wider range of participants, and many of the topics focused on the implications and desirability of research. Even so, there were few blacks and other minorities present. But the NIH, more politically confident than it had been earlier, footed the entire bill of $133,000.

One conclusion which was reached by consensus was that there is no gene for criminal behavior. But there was some agreement that there might be genes that predispose some people to engage in impulsive and compulsive behaviors, including violence.

II

The roots of public flare-ups over biology go back more than a century to the interpretation of Charles Darwin's theory of evolution. Various thinkers, beginning with Herbert Spencer in Britain in the late nineteenth century, fiddled with Darwin's theory and applied it to society, with horrific consequences. Spencer proposed that the fittest forms of societies advance, much like organisms, leaving the less fit behind. The idea supported the "rightful" dominance of Western culture, explaining away simpler societies and their "savages" as inferior.

On both sides of the Atlantic, during this time of industrial upheaval, urbanization, and social and economic inequities, "social Darwinism" developed into a conservative laissez-faire political agenda. In the United States, sociologist William Sumner even suggested, in *Folkways*, that poverty was the natural and direct result of biological inferiority.

Meanwhile, amateur psychologist Francis Galton, Darwin's cousin, began in 1869 to encourage an idea related to evolution: society could, and should, breed superior people. In 1883, he coined the term "eugenics," which he defined in *Inquiries into Human Faculty and Its Development* as "the science of improving stock." ("Eugenics" literally means "well-born.") One way to optimize societal evolution was to identify the best and the brightest of the most-developed societies and encourage them to have children.

The science tainted by such a racist philosophy included the turn-of-the-century study of criminals. It was widely accepted in the United States that immigrant groups had higher crime rates because of a flawed genetic inheritance. Henry Goddard, for one, believed that criminals were mentally inferior. He based this conclusion on a study of the hundreds of descendants of a soldier given the pseudonym Martin Kallikack.

Goddard researched two family lines: one began with Kallikack's son and a feeble-minded barmaid; the other track followed the children Kallikack had had with a Quaker woman, whom he had later married. Goddard reported that most of the descendants of the barmaid were criminals or "immoral" or feeble-minded. Of course, the Quaker woman's line produced normal and bright descendants. Goddard's research was based largely on gossip, as few of those "studied" were around to be assessed.

The temper of the times, which included a fierce belief in the moral obligation to stop the decline of society, also led to broad support in

North America and Europe for forced sterilization. The gene pool had to be kept as free as possible from criminality, mental illness and "moral degeneracy."

By the 1930s, some thirty U.S. states had compulsory-sterilization laws, aimed mostly at the insane and feeble-minded. These categories were sufficiently loosely defined to allow the inclusion of many immigrants and others who were functionally illiterate, who knew little or no English, and/or who performed poorly on intelligence tests. Some of the laws extended to sexual perverts, drug fiends, drunkards, epileptics and others deemed ill or degenerate. Tens of thousands of individuals were sterilized. In some states, this legislation remains on the books.

Eugenics peaked in the Nazi extermination programs. Killing of children who were physically and/or mentally disabled began in institutions in 1939. They were given lethal injections, poisoned, starved and/or gassed.

Jews, who were being blamed for Germany's economic setbacks, were quarantined in ghettos, ostensibly to prevent the spread of their "ill health." The "Jewish problem" was seen by Nazi eugenicists as a medical problem: Jews were pathological, diseased; therefore, they were confined to concentration camps and killed. The Nazis also applied their "selection and eradication" procedures to homosexuals, Gypsies, eastern European Slavs and other "undesirables."

The Nazi eugenics program drew, in part, on the work of scientists, doctors, academics and politicians in Britain and the United States. It was designed by "respectable" German scientists, doctors, academics and politicians involved in an ongoing dialogue with their American colleagues.

However, in the United States and Britain, even prior to the Nazi eugenics program, social Darwinism was being challenged. Some anthropologists, including Franz Boas and Ruth Benedict, were arguing that cultural patterns could account at least as well as eugenics for human group differences. The view that all societies pass through similar stages—a hallmark of social Darwinism—did not hold up.

This new wave of cultural anthropology would foster an interest in how culture made its mark on individuals. Psychologists who had been drawn by eugenics to study such things as racial differences in intelligence began to pay more attention to how individuals learned.

Although psychology had long entertained the idea that certain "instincts" or biological propensities contributed to, or even directed, behavior, the growing outcry against social Darwinism and eugenics made the study of instinct, indeed anything smacking of biology, lose much of its attraction. Still, some psychologists, such as Harry Harlow of the University of Wisconsin, didn't relegate instinct to the academic scrap heap. In 1958, Harlow published a study that suggested that learning theory, then in vogue in the study of both animals and humans, might not be sufficient to explain certain behavior.

Harlow constructed an experiment that tracked how infant rhesus monkeys reacted to a choice between two artificially created "mothers." One was constructed of wire but offered the infants milk. The other, a warm, terry-cloth creation, didn't offer milk. The infants chose the latter time after time, even though learning theory would lead one to predict that they would be given sufficient reinforcement from the milk "mother" to choose it instead.

Harlow got a mixed reaction from fellow psychologists. Some, no doubt, would have preferred to leave both instinct and biology alone; for others, however, Harlow's findings suggested that well-constructed experiments could offer clues to the role biology plays in behavior.

In the 1960s, instinct became the focus of a heated debate on the causes of violence. At one extreme was the claim that all violence resulted from an innate instinct expressed under the right social conditions. At the other was the belief that humans were born without any programming for violent behavior, that we learn to be violent.

This debate, which stretched through the 1970s, was sustained, in part, by several books that drew comparisons between animals and humans. These books advanced arguments based on the observation of animals, but were heavily indebted to Darwin's theory of evolution. Their authors' view was that the chances for reproductive success were increased by aggressive behavior. Aggression, in terms of the evolutionary spiral, was therefore not always destructive; it also served a constructive function in terms of adaptation and survival. Natural selection had programmed humans to be aggressive, both as part of their animal ancestry and in their own evolution as weapon-using hunters.

This point of view was the wellspring of the animal science, or ethology, of Konrad Lorenz, the author of *On Aggression*, published in 1963. Lorenz paid close attention to how birds, particularly geese, fight for dominance and territory. He also documented how they inhibit or channel aggression through ritual behavior involving threats and ceremonial displays. On the basis of these and other observations of animals, he concluded that the social order that emerges—the powerful males first in line—establishes a strong social structure that creates order, protects the weak and cares for the young.

Mainly, Lorenz concluded that the same biological processes are manifest in human culture, often played out in violent behavior, sadism, crime and war. As is true of other organisms, when inherited inhibitions break down, natural aggression finds expression in humans. Thus, Lorenz argued, overexposing children to the mass media's depictions of violence, including murder and war, might lessen inhibitions against committing violence. Similarly, crime and violence in big cities are related to the powerlessness of individuals, a condition that contributes to a violent climate.

According to Lorenz, not to acknowledge this instinct of violence is to deny one's evolutionary origins and to hinder self-knowledge. In a 1970 paper, he argued that "it is a truth and indubitably a moral postulate that all men should have an equal opportunity to develop. But an untrue dogma is easily derived from the truth that all men are potentially equal. The doctrine carries the premise one step further by asserting that man is born *tabula rasa* and that all his behavior is determined by 'conditioning.'" He called this a "pseudo-democratic doctrine," claiming that "biology has proven that men are not equal, identical, similar or anything of the sort, from the instant of conception." He suggested that this observation should be common sense to all.

Other books of mass appeal focused on the special bonds humans have with the animal kingdom. Their message, much like that of Lorenz, was that humanity had not yet divorced itself from evolution.

In 1967, Robert Ardrey, a dramatist and amateur anthropologist and ethologist, claimed in *The Territorial Imperative* that humans, like animals, stake out and defend territory because of an innate instinct. (This is, for example, how war occurs.) Also in 1967, Desmond Morris, a zoologist, wrote in *The Naked Ape* that humans were really only improved apes. Human behavior derives from apes' and is often similar in pattern.

The most heated reaction to Lorenz, Ardrey and Morris came from anthropologist Ashley Montagu. In his rebuttal in *The Nature of Human Aggression*, published in 1976, he condemned their comparisons of animal and human behavior as "gross extrapolations." He claimed, instead, that culture informs human behavior, that humans have a great capacity to learn and that most behavior credited to instinct is learned behavior. As evidence, he pointed to numerous examples of human cultures that place a high premium on cooperation, not on conflict. (According to historian Lewis Mumford, people began to make war only when they came to live in cities, around 5000 B.C.)

It is culture and social conditions that change human behavior, Montagu suggested. The ethologists were in way over their heads and should stick to watching birds and tending zoos.

While the early ethologists devised experiments in animal behavior and recorded their observations, the next generation of ethologists put on their hiking boots and went to live among the animals. The long-term study of natural habitats, particularly those of primates, has turned up a wealth of information about social behavior. Indeed, some data on the common features of animal and human life are of such high quality and so detailed that they are difficult to ignore.

Jane Goodall's study of chimp behavior is one such example. As she describes them in *The Chimpanzees of Gombe: Patterns of Behavior*, published in 1986, our primate cousins are not cute and cuddly creatures. They can be very violent, competitive and status-conscious, and they pursue dominance. Males expend considerable energy settling disputes, often by threat rather than battle. Goodall also observed that chimps hate strangers and patrol the boundaries of the group's territory. And, she noted, sometimes males behave as though they enjoy violence.

Such research helped fuel more social-scientific interest in biology in the 1970s. It encouraged "sociobiology," which, in its early days, focused primarily on how pressures exerted by animals' inherited traits and environments explained social behavior. Gone was the preoccupation with innate instincts. Genes might well be the prime movers, but they might be considered in the context of social fine-tuning.

The new crop of sociobiologists tend to call themselves "evolutionary psychologists." Peoples in all cultures, they propose, share an evolutionary concern with social status; they have a strong sense of justice, feel guilt in similar circumstances, and engage in reciprocal altruistic behavior. These deep ties are the glue of human culture, however culturally fine-tuned they may be. Genetic differences do not explain behavior; rather, behavior is the product of human nature— *the nature of all humans*.

In this view, violence is part of human structure. And humans may be violent in many places and on many occasions as a reaction to a threatening social environment.

Evolutionary psychology holds out the promise of liberating us from tenacious mind-versus-brain, them-versus-us thinking. It offers food for thought about how and why impoverished and conflict-ridden environments can provoke the violence in anyone.

On the other hand, it is still a young science and, as it is a science of human limits, it bears close scrutiny. We ultimately may find that we can appreciate some of these limits—we may become satisfied that they are fundamental to being human. However, perception of limits, as history reminds us, can become the stuff of political manipulation, racism and terror.

III

There is another stratum underlying the ongoing violence controversy. Brain surgery was performed in the 1960s in the hope of curing people of violence. Critics such as Breggin often cited these experiments as an example of how a biological approach to violence is premature, wrongheaded and ultimately inhuman.

At the time these experiments were being conducted, riots were destroying American cities, and anti-government sentiment was running high, particularly among minorities and college students. Breggin sees these experiments as the core of a first major U.S. government initiative to curb violence by intervening biologically, rather than through social policy that would target malnutrition, poverty and unemployment in the inner cities.

In order to understand the passions these experiments generated, we have to address the early history of the approach. In the early 1960s, neuropsychiatrist Frank Ervin and neurosurgeons Vernon Mark and William Sweet teamed up to conduct brain research at Boston's Massachusetts General Hospital, a Harvard affiliate. Early work by the group focused on how pain associated with cancer might be controlled by surgically blocking specific sites in the brain. This should be seen in the context of controversial experiments in brain surgery. (The relief of symptoms by brain changes rather than treatment of the cause of disease was usually referred to as "psychosurgery" when it was applied to a variety of mental disturbances.)

Surgically altering the brain has had a turbulent history. Experiments on chimps, first reported in 1935, showed that cutting into nerve fibers in the prefrontal lobes of the brain with a knife called a "leucotome," inserted into a hole drilled into the skull, appeared to relieve "frustrational behavior." Ignoring the numerous behavioral disabilities it caused the animals, the scientists decided to operate on humans— first on hospitalized patients suffering from "agitated depression" and chronic schizophrenia, then on the less disturbed.

"Prefrontal lobotomy," as the operation came to be known, often resulted in physical and mental disabilities. Moreover, the advocates of the procedure were often poorly trained, but strong self-promoters. By the mid-1950s, psychiatrists were discounting the leucotome procedure, as it was difficult to defend bad results and there were new, potentially better treatments, such as drugs and electroconvulsive therapy. By this time, however, U.S. surgeons, reacting, in part, to the demand for snappy postwar treatment of mentally traumatized soldiers, had performed some 50,000 prefrontal procedures.

Psychosurgery, however, did not die; it just got fancier. "Stereotaxic surgery" set out to destroy those brain areas thought to be associated with mental dysfunction. It involved plotting three coordinates on the head's surface as precise mathematical reference points, then using them to direct insulated electrodes to a target in the brain, and to record signals and stimulate the nerve fibers or burn them out. It was hoped that destroying tissue in a pinpointed target area would be less damaging than conventional surgery, which was very inexact and sometimes resulted in loss of memory and language.

Stereotaxic surgery was spurred on by the disappointing therapeutic results of psychiatry; during the mid-1960s, about 40,000 such procedures were carried out. One major target was the limbic region of the brain, long associated with the regulation of emotions. It was thought that this new form of surgery would ameliorate a wide range of disturbances, including aggression.

During this period, Ervin, Mark and Sweet were developing stereotaxic procedures as a treatment for temporal-lobe epilepsy. Ervin insists that they were not interested in psychosurgery, which treated symptoms. Rather, they hoped to correct the dysfunction in the brain, and thereby stop convulsive attacks. The experimental subjects were patients who had failed to respond well to anti-seizure medication and were referred to the group by neurologists. The testing phase of the new technique could last for days, even weeks. The surgeon administered mild electric currents via the electrodes implanted into the patient's brain. These stimulations revealed the precise areas of the brain that produced reactions approximating the patient's seizures. The surgeon then sent heat down the electrodes to burn the appropriate tissue. The results were promising, and in the course of these procedures, Ervin and his colleagues noticed that patients with temporal-lobe epilepsy also had histories of impulse-control loss and violent behavior. In fact, family members of some patients reported that violence was the most remarkable feature of the disorder. Stimulation of these areas of the brain was also found to produce such powerful effects as fear, sexual arousal and rage. It therefore appeared that temporal-lobe epilepsy and violent behavior were somehow elements of the same brain disease. In some patients, the surgery ended both seizures and violent behavior; in others, it blocked either the one or the other.

The procedure for temporal-lobe epilepsy may have paid an extra dividend—an important insight into the biology of violence. Might some out-of-control, violent individuals have abnormalities in the limbic region? This led to broader questions: How many violent people have some form of brain disease? Could violence be eliminated by medical means in some cases?

To begin answering these questions, Ervin set up a program in the Department of Psychiatry at Massachusetts General Hospital in conjunction with emergency services. Individuals who arrived at the hospital complaining of recurrent violence were often referred by doctors to Ervin's unit for an interview and a medical work-up. (Those who asked for help were not rare. Some even asked to be restrained because they felt a wave of violence coming on.) Of the 130 males studied, about 33 had temporal-lobe dysfunction. An equal number had symptoms—such as seeing an aura preceding a violent episode—also suggestive of a brain disorder.

The men studied were mostly working-class whites with a history of physical assaults, alcohol abuse, impulsive sexual behavior, auto accidents and moving traffic violations. Most were so terrified of their behavior that they had attempted suicide, in despair over injuries they had caused others. Most had had themselves committed to a mental institution at some time.

When Ervin took someone on as a patient, he immediately prepared commitment papers that were left undated. This ensured a ten-day stay in a state institution should a means of last-ditch control be needed.

Ervin also spent a lot of time on the telephone, trying to calm callers threatening suicide or violence to others and counseling those seeking help when they felt a violent episode was imminent. He would often be on the phone with a patient who was cowering in a corner or threatening to stab a spouse. The hospital even offered group therapy for the wives of these patients, encouraging them to leave home as soon as they sensed trouble brewing.

Many of the men were given the anticonvulsive drug Dilantin and responded well. Ervin would treat them as though they had seizures, and the drug would calm their propensity to violence. For example, after sustaining a head injury in a car crash, a previously loving and non-violent young professional man began to threaten his wife, slap his children and explode at work at the slightest provocation.

Head injuries can damage the undersurface of the brain's frontal lobe and the tips of the temporal lobe, elements of the limbic region that lie close to the bones of the skull. After a brain scan revealed irregularities, Ervin prescribed Dilantin and the man's violent behavior stopped.

Similarly, when a middle-aged policeman who crashed his motorcycle was subsequently released from hospital, it was thought he had no residual problems from the blow to his head. Yet, this kindly, jovial neighborhood cop soon began to have almost uncontrollable urges to kill everyone around him—and it terrified him.

About six months after his release from hospital, he would come home after work, fling his pistol across the room and handcuff himself to the bedstead. After his violent feelings passed, he would ask his wife to unlock him. The couple kept this behavior a secret. One evening, two co-workers were giving him a ride home when his problem surfaced. He dropped his gun in the front seat and chained himself to the prisoner's clip on the back door of the squad car. He pleaded with his friends not to tell anyone, but they brought him to the hospital emergency department. Tests showed he had a large blood clot and some underlying brain dysfunction. He underwent surgery, was put on Dilantin for a while, and was sent home. The violence had disappeared.

Ervin once received a call from a vice-president of a major corporation in South America who had somehow learned of his work and asked to meet with him at Logan Airport in Boston. During the short encounter, he revealed to Ervin that he was worried that his violent and bizarre sexual behavior would destroy him. He would, for example, find himself in an alley in São Paulo having sex with a twelve-year-old prostitute when he was supposed to be working. He was also becoming violent at home and was terrified that he would injure his wife. He lived in constant panic. Ervin prescribed Dilantin. A month later the patient wrote that he was no longer experiencing bizarre episodes.

In the mid-1960s, Ervin studied similar cases in prisons. One of the prisoners was serving two life terms for the rape and mutilation of two eight-year-old girls. He had even masturbated on their eviscerated intestines. The inmate explained to Ervin that, when this terrible feeling came over him, he would feel better only after he had committed a violent act.

To this point, Ervin and his colleagues had been quietly documenting how a subset of the population was violence-prone as a result of damage to the brain. However, a letter they sent to the *Journal of the American Medical Association* (*JAMA*) in 1967 made their views public. In it, they suggested that there were individuals who, if given half a chance, would find themselves striking out at others. Rioting by blacks in Roxboro, Massachusetts, and Newark, New Jersey, had given Ervin and his colleagues the idea that brain-damaged individuals might exploit times of social tension and upheaval to wreak havoc. While they acknowledged that poverty is the underlying cause of most riots, they wrote:

> It is important to realize that only a small number of the millions of slum dwellers have taken part in the riots and that only a sub-fraction of these rioters have indulged in arson, sniping and assault. Yet, if slum conditions alone determined and initiated riots, why are the vast majority of slum dwellers able to resist the temptations of unrestrained violence? Is there something peculiar about the violent slum dweller that differentiates him from his peaceful neighbor? . . . We need intensive research and clinical studies of the individuals committing the violence. The goal of such studies would be to pinpoint, diagnose, and treat those people with low violence thresholds before they contribute to further tragedies.

Adverse reaction to the letter came from many quarters, including Peter Breggin. In the minds of critics, Ervin, Mark and Sweet were simply targeting blacks. (Ervin admitted to me that writing such a letter at a time of social upheaval was both provocative and somewhat insensitive, but he stands by the message.) One critic wrote to *JAMA* suggesting that to rob people of violent expression would be to preclude responding with force against oppression.

In their rebuttal, the Harvard doctors advised against considering all violence to be the same: Failing to recognize the differences among types of violence was medical betrayal, irrespective of whether one believed violence should be morally advocated.

Peter Breggin now turned on what he believed to be a nascent program in behavior control. Mark and Ervin had written a book entitled *Violence and the Brain* in which they had described examples of temporal-lobe surgery that had subdued violent tendencies. They also suggested that this form of surgery might be of benefit to many people suffering from temporal-lobe epilepsy.

Breggin was horrified by the media's portrayal of Ervin, Mark and Sweet as having the solution to the growing violence. The June 21, 1968, issue of *Life*, for example, described their work as a young science that offered "insight and a potential of remedy for a worried society."

At this time, as part of the federal government's tougher stance on violence, plans involving NIMH and the Department of Justice were under way to explore genetic theories and to develop tests to identify individuals with violent tendencies and to initiate treatment programs, including drug therapies and behavior modification.

Breggin fanned the widespread flames of hostility toward both the government's plan and the views stated in *Violence and the Brain*. The government gradually backed off, and funding for biological studies shrank. Ervin's contract at Harvard was not renewed and he headed out to the University of California at Los Angeles, where he met with strong protests, from both students and faculty, against further violence research. At UCLA, he switched his focus to the study of primates (and continues this work in Montreal, at McGill University). Vernon Mark left Massachusetts General Hospital and was made chief of neurosurgery at Boston City Hospital.

But Breggin continued to seek to discredit one case characterized as a surgical success in *Violence and the Brain*. In the book, the patient was known as Thomas R. His real name was Leonard Kile.

When Ervin and Mark first met Kile, he was a thirty-four-year-old engineer who had developed seizures after injuring his head as a young adult. He began to have spells of rage: If a driver cut him off on the highway, he would pursue him, force his car to the side of the road and beat him up. If his wife seemed inattentive, he would throw her against a wall. Sometimes, his rage was directed at friends or co-workers. After each incident, he would be overcome with remorse.

Senior doctors at a Boston hospital could not treat Kile effectively and referred him to Ervin and Mark. When tests showed the type of electrical brain activity that is often indicative of epilepsy, and signs of other abnormalities, they decided to perform surgery. Though it failed to control Kile's epilepsy, he became less violent. According to Ervin, doctors had not been treating Kile for epilepsy, as they should have done, and he was going out of control. They were mistakenly treating him for symptoms of schizophrenia, which some temporal-lobe epileptics exhibit.

Kile was the inspiration for Michael Crichton's 1972 bestseller *The Terminal Man*. Crichton, a doctor, had observed the surgical procedure performed by Mark and wrote a fictional account of a patient who becomes crazed with violence after a badly botched experiment. Breggin held that the real-life surgery was a botch-job and accumulated a file charting Kile's delusional behavior, as evidenced in a series of hospitalizations. Breggin suggests that Kile was not as violent as Ervin and Mark made him out to be, and that surgery transformed a brilliant young engineer with marital problems into a demented and sporadically violent mental patient.

In 1973, Kile's mother, backed by the Church of Scientology, which supports actions against psychiatry, filed suit on his behalf, charging that he was permanently damaged as a result of the brain surgery. In 1979, Ervin and Mark were cleared of charges of malpractice.

Today, Ervin insists that he and Mark were the only ones to treat Kile appropriately. He claims that Breggin badly distorted their ideas and that Breggin's continuing challenge to a biological understanding of violence is drawing heavily upon political correctness, which condemns consideration of the most fundamental biological issues around violence. In a sensible society, Ervin says, if you are brain-damaged and in trouble with your behavior, you get help. In our society, you get shot, jailed or institutionalized.

Ervin says he is all for wiping out racism and poverty, but that there is no evidence that doing so would wipe out violence. And he's right. Even given the considerable limitations of modern scientific research, there is still sufficient evidence about how the brain can direct violence and how violence can be unleashed via cultural triggers to contradict simplistic social explanations of violence.

IV

Are the findings of violence research likely to be abused, either by government agencies or by grandstanding medical specialists? Most likely. Will those who suffer such abuse be the poor and members of minority groups? Most probably. Will violence research, on occasion, lead to some obvious politically motivated end? Certainly. This is the way of science and society—which is why patterns of research in this area must be vigilantly monitored by all of us.

But it would be folly to ignore or deny the value of research that potentially could lead us to greater self-knowledge, and perhaps wisdom, both personal and political.

The fact is, violence research is one of the major gateways to better understanding the brain. Already valuable insights have been gleaned, as we shall now discover.

3

Delicate Balance:

*How the Brain Appears to Direct Violence
and How Violence May Be Unleashed*

I

The heart seems to be everywhere. We revere it as symbolizing love ("I give you my heart"), courage ("she has heart") and hope ("take heart"). Similarly, characterizations such as "brainy" and "brainless" are casually tossed about, but usually we invoke that ephemeral entity the "mind" to explain our thoughts and decisions ("You have a mind, use it" or "I've lost my mind").

This doddering idea—that the human mind, attached but functioning separately from the body, is the engine of consciousness—has serious social consequences. It reinforces a social and, ultimately, political philosophy rooted in the onus of individual responsibility ("If you put your mind to it, you can live a decent life" or "Just say no"). Such extravagant faith in the power of the "mind" is typically used as a weapon to bludgeon individuals for their failure to achieve society's prevailing goals. If you are poor or violent, it must be *your* fault.

A competing idea holds that the human brain is the product of millennia of evolution, incorporating some 200 billion nerve cells and a supporting cast of at least a trillion other cells. This brain processes everything we experience in the outside world through its structures and chemistry. Unfortunately, we fail to appreciate how malleable the brain is, right from its embryonic development, and how vulnerable are its neural and chemical structures to damage and alteration. Such an understanding of the interplay of certain biological and environmental conditions would lead us to realize that *anyone* can become violent. We also ignore the pharmaceutical roulette we play with the brain's chemistry. Millions of us, in response to fashion and pharmaceutical promotional campaigns encouraged by physicians, think nothing of popping pills to make us more self-assured, brave or whatever. Yet too often we have only a poor understanding of how the addition of a powerful chemical to the already high-powered chemical factory of the brain can cause behavioral change, both short- and long-term.

The brain, the most complex living structure, is a mass of jelly-like pink-gray tissue encased in a tough membrane. It sits beneath the dome of the skull, positioned atop nerves descending the spine to every region of the body. It may be only the size of a small grapefruit, consist mainly of water and weigh somewhere between 2.5 and 3 pounds, but it is the body's control center.

The brain is not likely to win beauty pageants, but it is endlessly fascinating. For instance, take the brain's quarter-inch-thick wriggly cap, the "cortex." Only 250,000 years old, it's the newest part of the brain, enabling us to process concepts and perceptions, to be "self-aware."

This "smart" cap is the outer layer of the cerebrum, the largest part of the brain. The cerebrum comprises the right and left hemispheres, separated by the "corpus callosum," a thick bundle of fibers. Each hemisphere is divided into four lobes.

The largest, the frontal lobes, are involved in the processing of thought, including the human ability to foresee the consequences of behavior. The temporal lobes are involved in hearing, memory and our sense of time and self. The occipital lobes process vision. The parietal lobes deal with such body senses as touch and pressure.

At the bottom of the brain, at the very back, is the cerebellum, the "little brain," primarily concerned with the coordination of muscular movement.

Deeper in the brain is the 400-million-year-old region often referred to as the "limbic system." It thrived some 150 million years ago, when our reptilian ancestors ruled the planet. Its structures and functions, modified through evolution, connect to most parts of the brain and incorporate some of the upper portions of the brain stem, the most primitive part of the brain, which regulates such basic human mechanisms as heart rate.

Neuroscience long considered the limbic system as the center of our sex drive and emotions—joy, pleasure, pain, fear and rage. Of late, however, there has been some debate about which structures in this region actually play an important role in certain emotions. For example, recent New York University research on rat-brain signals suggests that the almond-shaped structure known as the "amygdala" appears to play a key role in the regulation of fear. Neuroscientist Joseph LeDoux carefully tracked a sound stimulus (intended to cause fear). It entered the brain and traveled along a neural pathway to the thalamus, a kind of relay station for almost all information, and then directly to the amygdala. Severing this pathway made it impossible for the rats to learn to fear the sound.

In his 1996 book, *The Emotional Brain*, LeDoux contends that, once human emotions are processed via the amygdala, they may sometimes be difficult to turn off. For example, when a strong signal is processed, it can potentially unleash a "fight or flight" alert. (Animals such as cats will either flee or attack, depending on the conditions they find themselves in.) In humans, he suggests, while the amygdala responds quickly to a threat, and thus provokes an emotional response, the individual's higher cortex, or thinking brain, will receive the same stimulus more slowly from the thalamus, making it difficult, under certain conditions, to stop the amygdala's alarm system. Does this mean that emotions may sometimes rule when there is a perceived threat? Does this mean that controlling emotions may sometimes be difficult? Yes.

As Vernon Mark and Frank Ervin explain in *Violence and the Brain*, it appears that there exists within the brain a neural process that organizes effective and directed attack behavior. The product of a long evolutionary past, it emerged as necessary for survival.

Evolution demands that we acknowledge our common biological

past with other vertebrates. Part of that past involves the potential for violence. Animal and clinical experiments have shown that the core of that potential, as well as mechanisms to inhibit violence, are present in the limbic region of the brain.

In species after species, ethologists report, fighting often becomes ritualized. For example, Jane Goodall's research on the behavior of chimps at Gombe National Park in Tanzania shows that they settle disputes mainly by threats. This suggests the existence of a circuit breaker that prevents violence; for, when fighting does ensue, it can be vicious.

In humans, evolution appears to have put emotional regulation largely under the final control of the cortex, the cap of reasoning, embodying the forces of socialization and culture. This does not mean, however, that the dark emotions humans are capable of expressing have been tamed.

Though the mapping of structures in the brain has become increasingly sophisticated, our understanding of many of these brain areas is rudimentary, a fact that resurfaces with each new adventure into high-tech brain research. Of late, for example, use of powerful imaging devices that take snapshots of the brain in action has produced some intriguing, if preliminary, results. One study revealed that women utilize eight times more brain area when they become sad than do men. Women, it appears, show more activity in the "cingulate gyrus," which encloses the limbic ring, an area of the brain involved with speech processes. It has therefore been suggested that this may be the reason why women tend to express emotion through words. Men, when they are sad, show more activity in the limbic-temporal area, which is associated with aggression.

That it is very intriguing is about as much as anyone should at present declare on the subject; the research is too new, the computer-driven imaging technology too inexact, and the brain too complex for cocky absolutism.

It is suggested rather self-servingly by those who oppose biological research on violence that the brain is simply beyond human comprehension. The fact is, however, that we do have some general idea of how the brain works and we are rapidly accumulating enough research information to posit—and support—some clever theories.

And what is the prevailing theory of how the brain works? The answer, based on extensive research over decades, involves tiny cells and chemicals.

The brain is principally a massive communications system. Comprising only about 2 percent of our body weight, it absorbs about 15 percent of the body's blood supply and about 25 percent of its oxygen. It is driven by billions of gray cells called "neurons," which form trillions of connections, and by chemicals called "neurotransmitters," which carry messages. Some fifty of these chemicals have been identified, but there may be a hundred or more.

As sensory information comes into the brain, neurons churn out electrical signals via club-like projections called "axons." These axons do not actually connect to other neurons; a near-invisible gap called a "synapse" is bridged electrochemically. Neurons, which manufacture the neurotransmitters, actually spray them across the space to gateways (called "receptors") on other neurons. It is argued that the overall result of this electrical and chemical tide in the brain, involving huge numbers of neurons and their neurotransmitters, is consciousness. Changes in the way we think and feel will occur as the gateways on neurons react to the rise and fall of neurotransmitter chemicals, which lead the neurons to change the rates of the signals they send out.

How does this extraordinary enterprise hang together? In brain science, this is known as the "binding question."

One hypothesis of how the brain works was proposed in a 1993 paper by New York University neuroscientist Rudolfo Llinàs. Armed with some supporting experimental evidence, including the results of recent animal-brain experiments at Laval University in Quebec City, he holds that regular and rapidly occurring cycles of nerve impulses from the brain's thalamus scan the entire brain and trigger synchronized cells that record sensory data at the particular time and at a particular electrical rhythm. The responses from these cells account for a brief flicker of consciousness. Because this process occurs so fast, constantly updating and processing sensory information, consciousness appears continuous. In short, the theory suggests that what we refer to as "mind" is actually time-coded interplay between the thalamus and cerebral cortex, as the body interacts with its surroundings.

Another view is offered by University of Iowa neuroscientist Antonio Damasio, author of *Descartes' Error*. He theorizes that consciousness emerges as a result of the ability of certain areas in the brain's prefrontal cortex (he calls them "convergence zones") to process representative images of thought, memory, emotion and experience. When these brain regions are damaged, as his numerous clinical cases reveal, decision making, which, for example, normally involves both thought and emotion, becomes difficult.

Other brain explorers, such as philosopher Daniel Dennett, contend that it takes the activity of the entire brain to produce consciousness. Dennett suggests that the brain, in dealing simultaneously with many sequences of computations, rather than a single sequence, produces changing versions of what we call "experience" or "the self."

Further insight into how the brain works has been gleaned from research into the dream state. Allan Hobson, a neuroscientist at Harvard University, holds that input from the outside world is shut out when certain brain chemicals sprayed from neurons in the brain stem overpower the chemicals that keep the brain alert. When this occurs, self-awareness is interrupted. Experiences drawn, probably at random, from within the brain by still-functioning higher cell networks are likely to be fragmented, if not exotic or outlandish—in other words, dreams.

Both types of brain theory—of binding and of dreaming—are likely to be revised again and again, as we should expect of science; but the theories also indirectly counsel that human experience can be—and usually is—very malleable.

II

Some research links physical and chemical changes in the brain to violence. This body of knowledge, although still in its infancy, is often sufficiently sophisticated to warrant serious consideration.

One of the most convincing scientific findings is that head

injuries, which can cause damage to the brain, appear to contribute to violence. In one study, by psychiatrist Dorothy Lewis, every one of the fourteen juveniles on death row had suffered a serious head injury in childhood; each had been physically abused. In another study of ninety-seven juveniles in jail and twenty-nine on death row, she found a common profile of abuse, bruises on the brain, and neurological problems such as learning disabilities, seizures and low IQ. Lewis contends that abuse coupled with neurological problems heightens the probability of violence. Brain damage, as she contends, may make it more difficult to control rage. (Inflicting head injuries can lead to laceration of the white nerve fibers that link the prefrontal cortex to deeper brain structures thought to be involved in the generation of aggressive impulses; the prefrontal lobes inhibit those impulses.)

In a recent study, California researchers tracked 4,269 males from birth through age eighteen. They found that birth trauma, including forceps delivery, plus a mother's loveless reaction to the child, increases threefold the risk of committing robbery, assault or murder. The assumption, again, is that neurological damage somehow unleashes a propensity toward violent behavior.

Brain functions may be disrupted by a blow to the head. Even a relatively mild shaking of an infant's head will bounce the brain around in the cranium. There is evidence that small hemorrhages will appear and that the resulting subtle neurological abnormalities will affect learning ability. This condition is sometimes referred to as "minimal brain dysfunction."

Severe blows to the head may destroy neurons. If enough axons are sheared, thus affecting neuron-to-neuron communication, coma may occur. The punch-drunk fighter comes to mind here. Experience with football players who receive numerous knocks reveals there may even be permanent memory loss.

Each year, at least 400,000 Americans are hospitalized with a brain injury. Car accidents account for almost 50 percent of the cases; falls, 21 percent; firearms, 12 percent; and sports, 10 percent. Very little is currently known about the long-term impact of these injuries.

Based on his clinical experience, psychiatrist Frank Ervin notes that other influences, too, may figure in causing brain injury: for example, viral encephalitis produces mental aberrations, sexual overindulgence and violent outbursts. The virus infects the temporal lobe of the brain and can have some impact on the hippocampus, a structure in the limbic region. Other brain infections associated with violent behavior include fungal meningitis, syphilis and herpes simplex.

A tumor or cyst in the limbic region or its connections may also lead to violence; a tumor in the pineal gland deep in the skull can lead to explosive behavior. And, as Damasio's research shows, other parts of the brain, when damaged, can cut off the emotions. One of his patients, a businessman who had a brain tumor in the prefrontal cortex, was no longer capable of experiencing emotion after surgery.

Some potent drugs, such as "angel dust," cocaine and amphetamines, may destabilize the brain, as may toxic substances, including metals absorbed from air pollution, paint and foods. One major culprit in causing brain damage is lead, which particularly affects learning abilities; as well, a recent study at the University of Pittsburgh Medical Center revealed that chronic low-level exposure to the metal is also associated with aggressive behavior. A poor diet, low in iron and calcium, may raise levels of lead in the body. Lead poisoning disproportionately affects black children living in the inner cities of the United States.

A number of brain-related medical conditions—stroke, multiple sclerosis, Alzheimer's and temporal-lobe epilepsy—appear to facilitate violence in individuals who, prior to becoming ill, show little sign of recurrent aggression.

All these examples of brain damage and its link to violence show how the stability of the brain can be profoundly altered by quite small lesions at specific sites. Ervin suggests that *any* damage to the brain alters its neurochemistry. The result is that the regulatory hold of the cortex on emotions may be relaxed, and violent behavior may occur. An impairment of the cortex or an irritation or stimulation of the amygdala can potentially cause such a change.

Research has linked certain neurotransmitters in the brain to violence; some has focused on how environmental stimuli can change the levels of these chemical supplies. Most engaging are data suggesting that threatening environments, including impoverished ones and those in which there is abuse or neglect in early childhood, may change brain chemistry into a mode that makes violent behavior more likely.

The neurotransmitter that violence researchers have studied the most, thus far, is serotonin (known chemically as 5-Hydroxytryptamine). The building-block of serotonin is the amino acid L-tryptophan, which is not produced in the body: it is consumed in foods such as grains, potatoes, bananas and turkey. The tryptophan is released during digestion and is carried by the blood to the brain and certain neurons in the brain stem; it is then converted, with the help of enzymes, into serotonin.

Serotonin is not an all-purpose neurotransmitter, but it is involved in such basic operations as control of body temperature, cardiovascular function and respiration. Its high profile comes from its association with such powerful experiences as courage, self-worth, some mental illnesses and violence.

Serotonin neurons, though relatively few in number, form a network that reaches almost every part of the central nervous system. Indeed, it forms the broadest-based electrochemical system in the brain.

Serotonin was discovered in the body in the mid-1950s, and in brain cells a decade later. It has been studied extensively in animals, and the results overwhelmingly indicate that a low supply of it is associated with violent behavior. A typical finding in monkeys, for example, is that those with low serotonin are more likely than those with a regular supply of the chemical to be aggressive, to bite and chase others. One monkey study also suggests those with low levels may be unable to form close relationships.

Numerous human studies since the 1970s also show that signs of low serotonin concentrations in the blood or spinal fluid correlate with aggressive, impulsive behavior. In a recent study in Finland, impulsively violent individuals who have committed murder or attempted murder were found to have low levels of serotonin. And in one recent study of twenty-nine problem children, low serotonin was the best predictor of which ones would commit violent crimes or suicide.

Other studies, including post-mortem brain measurements of serotonin, have linked a low supply of the chemical to suicide and to planned suicide attempts by adults in hospitals. Another study found that an inherited gene variant in people predisposed to suicide while drunk was related to low serotonin release, especially in the frontal lobes of the brain.

Some preliminary studies suggest that stressful environments lower signs of serotonin in some individuals. To determine how this occurs will require painstaking science; however, early hints are appearing in the scientific literature.

One animal study at the University of Massachusetts is very revealing. It involved golden hamsters, which have the same behavior-regulating brain chemicals as humans do. Normally these animals are friendly household pets, but when they were placed in stressful environmental conditions, they developed the potential to be killers. The hamsters were put into cages at an early age with older hamsters, who continually threatened, and even attacked them. When these victimized hamsters were then put into cages with smaller, weaker hamsters, they attacked them. The study showed that the early stress they had suffered had disrupted the brain circuitry that produced two brain chemicals involved in the regulation of violence—serotonin and vasopressin. The effects appeared to be lasting.

The study raises the question of whether children who have stressful and violent childhoods may also develop permanently faulty brain chemistry that predisposes them to violence. Living in poverty, perhaps in proximity to crackhouses, gunfights and muggings, may negatively affect an individual's serotonin and vasopressin levels. If current research on brain chemicals holds, we may find that a stress-ridden life presents a major biological challenge to the brain's stability and its mechanisms for inhibiting violence. Some individuals might be especially vulnerable, as genetics may play a role in the amount of serotonin converted from tryptophan. Indeed, a preliminary study by American researchers at the National Institutes of Health has identified a gene that may help keep serotonin levels low.

Recent long-range studies of groups of children who had stressful childhoods suggest that this brain-chemistry research is on track. Overall, data show that childhood victims of abuse and neglect are usually the most violent as teenagers. One ten-year University of Montreal study showed that such individuals from the inner city were more often involved in violent crimes, and indirect measurement of their serotonin levels revealed them to be lower than those of non-aggressive individuals.

Stress before birth may also have a negative impact. In humans, it has long been known that maternal stress or minor infections during pregnancy can affect the offspring. Brain circuits are highly malleable *in utero* as they begin to form networks and build stability.

The brain continues to be changeable and vulnerable to stress well into adulthood. Research conducted at the Veterans Affairs Medical Center in West Haven, Connecticut, demonstrates that severe emotional trauma experienced by soldiers has been linked to shrinkage of the hippocampus, a sea horse–shaped brain structure vital to learning and memory. It is believed that hormones that flood the brain to mobilize it in the face of a threat can be toxic to cells in the hippocampus. A similar finding has been reported in women who had been sexually abused in childhood. However, it is not yet clear whether some individuals are more susceptible to these changes and/or whether they originally had a smaller-than-normal hippocampus.

Brain research is also ongoing to determine whether serotonin levels can be altered by diet. Early investigations focused on the possibility that a supplemented diet of tryptophan would have a calming effect on otherwise volatile individuals. Frank Ervin and his colleagues at McGill University studied aggressive schizophrenic patients who were incarcerated in a hospital for mentally ill offenders. All had been convicted of murder or other person-related crimes. All behaved in a threatening and aggressive manner and had responded very poorly to traditional psychiatric medication. When supplemental tryptophan was administered, individuals who were impulsive showed positive results. Others, however, did not benefit from the tryptophan, leaving the researchers to investigate for the conditions under which the therapy does work.

Recent research at the University of Texas reinforces some of the Montreal findings. The study of ten healthy men showed that a low-tryptophan diet correlated with more aggressive behavior when they played a game that allowed them to earn money. As in the Montreal research, the diet did not affect everyone in the same way. Some of the men were more aggressive than others, suggesting that they were more prone to the effect of serotonin-lowering. At Yale University, seventeen adults with autism were involved in a similar study. The low-tryptophan diet led to a major increase in aggressive behavior, such as pacing, whirling and hitting oneself.

Though the focus in studies has been mainly on serotonin, there has also been increasing interest in another neurotransmitter, noradrenaline, the "alarm hormone." It organizes the brain to respond to danger. A monkey study at the University of Wisconsin found that noradrenaline levels can be elevated in a fetus when its mother is exposed to the stress of loud noise. After birth, these monkeys were more impulsive and overresponsive than normal ones. As they got older, their noradrenaline levels remained high and they continued to be hostile and aggressive

Much like the Wisconsin monkey study, the few human studies suggest that mothers who report high levels of stress during pregnancy tend to have hyperactive and learning-delayed babies. High noradrenaline levels have been reported in inner-city children, in war veterans, and in some of the children who were members of the Branch Davidian cult that was destroyed in Waco, Texas.

On the other hand, individuals with low noradrenaline levels appear to be more than usually inclined to take calculated risks or become thrill seekers. There is also suggestive case-study evidence that low noradrenaline types can be "cold-blooded" killers.

And what about testosterone? Is it the raging hormone that fires up aggressive behavior? The chemical associated with machismo? Scientific studies can't find much evidence of it. In fact, research at the University of California at Los Angeles shows that those men who have a *deficiency* of testosterone tend to feel aggressive and irritable. When given supplemental therapy, they sometimes become quite calm and friendly.

Ironically, it appears that the female hormone estrogen, which men have in low levels, may contribute to violence. Research at the University of Pennsylvania suggests that an increase in teen aggression—both male and female—may be related to estrogen. When girls whose onset of puberty was delayed were given estrogen therapy, the increase was noted. Boys late in sexual maturation were given testosterone; they achieved an equal level of aggression only with their last and highest dose. Why the delay? According to the researchers, much of the testosterone available to the brain is converted to estrogen. This process takes longer to affect behavior than did the direct injection of estrogen that the girls received.

While all these studies of brain chemistry suggest that biology is important to the understanding of our potential for violence, it is also evident that there is a complex relationship between physical markers and environmental inputs; this is a pivotal feature of violence that we cannot afford to continue to ignore.

III

It appears that physical or chemical changes to the brain trigger processes that facilitate violence. The range of inputs that can help make this happen, however, seems to be quite broad—from blows to the head to chronic environmental stress and threat. Research efforts to unravel these processes have been hampered by the numerous variables that can come into play.

Unfortunately, the aim of much of the research is to try to find the "cause" of violence, as if violence were a disease that could be treated, if not cured. Such a premise leads to the misdirected hope that a simple biological sign or marker will be discovered that predicts which individuals are "destined" to become violent. Find the marker, the reasoning goes, initiate a therapy, and the "patient" will be "treated." This approach ignores environmental influences on biology and behavioral settings, and assumes that violence and related emotions can be calmed solely—and safely—through pharmaceutical engineering. Two such medical approaches that deserve special mention involve the increased use of

Prozac, an antidepressant, to rejig serotonin levels in the brain, and the use of supplemental nutrients to lessen a propensity for violence.

Prozac is, of course, the wonder drug of the 1990s, the "smart drug" featured on the cover of *Newsweek*. It is even enthusiastically endorsed by some doctors for individuals who wish to gain self-confidence. Many Prozac users claim the drug has changed—or even saved—their lives. Little wonder that Prozac has become the world's leading antidepressant, generating more than $2 billion annually for its manufacturer, Eli Lilly.

The company claims that Prozac will prevent brain cells from reabsorbing used serotonin. This means more serotonin is available to receptors in the brain. Higher serotonin levels have been associated by many psychiatrists, and their patients, with feelings of enhanced security, courage, self-worth, serenity and resilience. More than 20 million people have tried Prozac.

However, in 1990 a Harvard psychiatric team reported on six patients who developed "intense, violent suicidal preoccupations" within two to seven weeks of starting Prozac treatment. The report estimated that between 1.9 and 7.7 percent of patients on Prozac would have suicidal thoughts at some point during treatment. The report drew support from some psychiatrists, but was widely criticized for not taking into account that four of the suicidal patients were also on other medications.

Three years later, after the Harvard team documented similar cases, the U.S. Food and Drug Administration, which is responsible for monitoring drug safety and efficacy, required that Lilly change Prozac's label to include reports of associated suicide and violent behavior. The FDA, however, decided there was insufficient scientific evidence to declare Prozac a problem drug.

The fact is that there are no long-term data on the effects of Prozac on the brain. (Indeed, the FDA approves most drugs for market on the basis of relatively short-term safety data.) It is very worrisome, given what science is discovering about the relationship between serotonin and violence, and about the complexity of the relation of overall brain chemistry to violence.

How might Prozac trigger violence or self-destructive behavior, considering the drug is said to raise, not lower, serotonin levels?

Psychiatrist Peter Breggin theorizes that the brain may react to Prozac by trying to keep a natural balance of its supply of the chemical. It may shut down production of serotonin to offset Prozac's ability to block the removal of used serotonin by those same neurons. The result might be an initial dip in overall available serotonin, which, in turn, might facilitate violent or self-destructive behavior.

According to this scenario, as exposure to Prozac continues, an increasing number of serotonin receptors on neurons may lose function, and even disappear, thereby keeping serotonin in neurons in chronically low supply. Research is still required to clarify this issue; but, as Prozac has become a cash cow for the manufacturer and there is strong psychiatric support for the drug, there appears to be little incentive or pressure to investigate fully.

Quite apart from its effect on serotonin levels, however, there is another reason to be wary of Prozac: it may not stay clear of other brain chemicals. To date, very little is understood about the relationship between brain chemistry and the body's hormonal system. The fact that a drug such as Prozac has been so widely introduced into this mysterious landscape, without well-controlled, long-term studies, is troubling. The financial engines driving pharmaceutical markets and the public obsession with magic bullets may override the reservations of appropriate science and cautious medicine.

Further studies are required on the potential cancer-promoting effects of Prozac and other antidepressants, as preliminary studies at the University of Manitoba suggest that there is such a hazardous link. And studies are also required to determine to what extent Prozac may create dependency.

There is, however, a more basic question concerning the ability of Prozac to do what the hype claims. A "meta-analysis" study published in October 1994 in the *Journal of Nervous and Mental Disease* showed that Prozac is no more effective than the older generation of antidepressants. (Meta-analyses combine statistics from many small studies into a large one; the approach is thought to provide a more accurate assessment of a medical treatment than any single study.) It concludes that Prozac "produces modest effects, roughly comparable in magnitude to those of other antidepressants."

Despite such concerns, Zoloft and Paxil, serotonin-related drugs similar to Prozac, have recently appeared on the market, and about twenty others are in development. By 1998, it is estimated that this market will be worth $6 billion annually.

In the popular media, from magazines to talk shows, these days someone always seems to be celebrating his or her changed personality, thanks to the new chemistry. Some true believers, particularly psychiatrists, mention only in passing that medicine has much to learn about these drugs. Yet medicine has even more basic lessons to learn about the brain and how its complex chemical balancing act is affected by any intruding chemical agent.

It is educational to observe that our culture is both bent on salvation through brain drugs—presumably because drugs are promoted as having a direct, predictably beneficial impact on brain chemistry—and convinced that individuals are responsible for their actions. This lack of logic may be linked to the widespread belief in a mind or soul separate from the brain. It is acceptable to manipulate the brain in order to change personality, because the "mind," the brain's organizer, remains in separate, and ethical, control.

In California, a different kind of medical fix is being pursued. The push comes from an oil and real estate millionaire who has been relying on intriguing, yet marginal, brain science to advance his belief in a marker for violence.

Everett "Red" Hodges became preoccupied with violence because his younger son, Todd, had been episodically violent and hyperactive, and had learning disabilities, and Lance, the older son, was almost killed during a mugging. The mugger had broken his victim's nose, knocked his teeth out and fractured his skull. He got $60. It had taken three brain operations and three months in hospital to clean out the blood clots.

Wanting to find reasons for violence, Hodges and his wife, Mary, set up a research foundation; its first study was to analyze hair samples from violent criminals. In his search for answers to Todd's problems, he had come across research that found abnormal levels of trace elements and toxic metals in the hair of children with behavioral and learning problems. Several reports suggested that hair analysis could be useful in differentiating violent people from the non-violent.

As he has many political connections, Hodges convinced the State of California, beleaguered by overcrowded prisons and violent crime, to make an exception to its ban on using prisoners as experimental subjects.

Hodges turned to Louis Gottschalk, chairman of the Department of Psychiatry at the University of California at Irvine, to conduct the research. Gottschalk is a veteran researcher and has published scores of articles in respected journals. He had not been very impressed by the rigor of hair-analysis research, but he agreed to undertake Hodges's study, thinking that he might improve upon the methodology.

The first study was conducted in 1984 on the hair of men who had been incarcerated for violent acts, including rape, battery and murder. The results surprised both Gottschalk and Hodges. They had assumed, on the basis of previous research, that the results might show high levels of metals such as lead, cadmium and copper; but it was manganese levels that appeared to be significantly elevated.

All three groups of prisoners Gottschalk had studied—thirty-nine whites, thirty-three Hispanics and thirty-two blacks—at a state prison in Stanislaus, California, had high levels of manganese in their hair. Two felony-free control groups—guards from the prison and locals approached at barber shops for hair samples—did not.

This was curious. Normally, the body regulates the intake, distribution and excretion of manganese very efficiently. It is a common metal, found in water, soil and air, and in such foods as wheat, rice and tea.

It is known that, when humans are exposed to high levels of the metal, they may experience hallucinations as well as the tremors and muscular rigidity common in Parkinson's disease. There are numerous scientific reports of these effects occurring in workers in mines and at manufacturing and welding plants. Biochemical analysis of brain tissue of humans and monkeys poisoned by manganese shows it plays a role in the death of brain cells, and may even influence the development of progressive neurologic diseases such as Huntington's, Alzheimer's, and amyotrophic lateral sclerosis (Lou Gehrig's disease).

Gottschalk, however, was not satisfied that the study was properly controlled. With backing from Hodges, he repeated the study twice, in 1987 and 1988. Hoping to eliminate any possible factors attributable to prison life, such as residue from cooking utensils, he studied eighty-nine violent male prisoners awaiting trial in Los Angeles and San Bernardino County jails.

In the follow-ups, Gottschalk also instituted better controls for factors such as age and race. And he took further precautions to ensure that the hair samples were not contaminated.

The results of the first study held up and, in 1991, Gottschalk published details of the three studies in the journal *Comprehensive Psychiatry*.

For Gottschalk, the research, while intriguing, had not proven a link between manganese and violence. At most, the metal appeared to be a "marker" that consistently showed up in people who were convicted of violent crimes. Perhaps it was playing some role in violence; but further research would have to address this possibility. Studies would have to focus on, say, hockey players or boxers who were aggressive but had no criminal history.

As well, very little information had been gathered about the backgrounds of the violent prisoners and the controls, or if exposure to manganese differed between the groups. Gottschalk also knew that the concentration of manganese in hair didn't indicate how much was in the blood or brain.

Nonetheless, Hodges used the results as an indication that it might soon be possible to run tests in the prison system, pull out the violent inmates identified on the evidence of the marker and treat them. Hodges immediately set out to find a way to neutralize the high levels of manganese and any other toxic metals in the hair of violent prisoners.

To this end, he sponsored a study by Stephen Schoenthaler, a researcher in nutrition and behavioral disorders at Stanislaus College. The study, launched in 1991, was to determine whether violence in prisoners, as measured by the reported numbers of violent incidents they committed in jail, could be reduced by changing their body chemistry via a supplemental diet of vitamins and minerals. The state once again gave Hodges its permission to experiment on the inmates.

The study focused on men from two California youth correctional facilities; 449 male volunteers were involved, aged eighteen to twenty-five. They were randomly assigned to a group receiving a placebo, a standard vitamin–mineral formula, or to a group receiving three times that amount. The "double-blind" research had been designed so that neither Schoenthaler and his associates nor the prisoners knew which treatment each individual received for a period of fifteen weeks.

The results showed that only the group given the standard formula had engaged in significantly fewer incidents of violence—46 percent fewer than the recorded baseline level. This group also had 58 percent fewer reports of non-violent incidents in jail. Further analysis revealed that 17 percent of those in this group had dramatically contributed to the overall result, suggesting that some prisoners had responded much better to the vitamin–mineral formula than had others.

In a preliminary report that Schoenthaler sent to Hodges, he claimed that the standard formula had "normalized" those who had reduced their level of violence in jail—a very strong claim, given that there are no established scientific standards for "normal." Nor had the study attempted to compare how body chemistry had changed after placebo or treatment.

California prison officials who had cooperated in the study weren't entirely pleased with the handling of the experimental procedures. But a moderately supportive evaluation of the study's findings by an out-side statistician persuaded Hodges that he had a potential therapy to treat violence. He even suggested making nutrient-supplementation a condition of probation and parole; regular testing would ensure compliance. The state, he estimated, would save millions of dollars by curbing recidivism and violent crime.

There is certainly little doubt that a strong relationship exists between diet and brain functioning. Studies show, for example, that malnourished animals become apathetic, irritable and fearful, and have a heightened startle response. As well, memory, abstract reasoning and verbal skills are subpar in severely malnourished children. It has also been noted that children who die of malnutrition have fewer brain cells than do children who eat normally. However, behavioral changes brought about by better nutrition are difficult to sustain without enrichment of one's environment; social factors are part of the equation.

As for the role of manganese in violence, research in animals shows that it can lower serotonin levels in the brain, and can accumulate in the same brain regions as the enzyme monoamine oxidase A, or MAOA. Manganese, it seems, can increase levels of the enzyme, and this action can trigger biochemical processes that ultimately reduce serotonin levels.

As intriguing as this early science may appear, it is hardly the basis for a violence-intervention program.

IV

Our understanding of violence will not be broadened if we become fixated on finding cures for it. It is not likely that one biological factor or syndrome explaining violence can be isolated. If anything, the available science tells us that the potential for violence is part of the human condition, the legacy of a very long evolutionary history that is within each of us. This is fundamental "wiring," although it will play out differently in each individual: Your response to a threat will not necessarily be my response, but each of us *will* respond to the threat. The nature of that response will be culturally and politically appraised in the context of society's rules at that time. For example, if you live in an impoverished urban neighborhood, you may deduce from your experience that carrying a gun is vital for protection and survival. As well, you may be convinced that replying to a perceived threat by using a gun will ensure your survival. Mainstream society certainly won't agree with your perception of your situation, but a biological marker that would predict that you are likely to react violently to a threat would miss the point. In evolutionary terms, using a gun in certain environments is, indeed, likely to increase your odds of staying alive.

What can be gleaned from the current research trends in the biology of violence is this: As much as we intellectually abhor bloodshed and cruelty, each human brain is capable of unleashing this violence. There are processes in the brain that usually keep this potential in check; but there are many ways in which this delicate balance can be tipped. There is no escape from the human potential for behaving violently.

What is extremely difficult to determine is when, if ever, medicine should intervene. This is not simply a medical question, but also a political one that has been inadequately debated. Sadly, in our hell-bent-on-law-and-order approach to violence, wholesale medical intervention may appear to be noble and humane. This is as dangerous as it is alluring.

It will likely take a long time for our culture to accept that violence may only be a bunch of firing neurons away. Brain science will not soon turn the tables on the mind. And society is still very much preoccupied with violence, as though it were something that visits us from without. The focus remains very much on the atrocities committed by "them" on "us."

In order to help the cause of the brain, let us focus more attention, in the next part of this book, on the violence of everyday life, the common violence that turns our personal worlds upside down. It's there and easily observed.

2

FORMS OF VIOLENCE

4
Everyday Violence:

Reaching the Breaking Point

I

Look at yourself in a mirror and consider the essence of what you are seeing. Do you believe that deep within you resides a soul that is imprinted with your personality traits, a kind of power plant existing beyond time and space? Or can you comfortably entertain the idea that the self-image that makes you feel unique and separate from others is the result of ongoing interaction between brain and environment; that it is being modified moment to moment by the neurons and message-carrying chemicals in the brain?

Our belief that each of us has a durable "self" and the capacity for "self-control" is reinforced by our highly developed potential to anticipate and plan a future, courtesy of the human brain's enlarged frontal lobes. Our culture ignores this self-deception by promoting the notion that we can indeed control the "self" at will, if we put our minds to it. Many people have even accepted the postulate that fighting life's "evil temptations" will be rewarded in the hereafter.

The assumption that we have enormous, if not unlimited, potential for "self-control" was strongly reinforced during the industrial and political revolutions of the eighteenth century, which gave rise to utopian visions of a peaceful world created through the exercise of reason.

Because we have come to view ourselves as "civilized," we have dissociated ourselves from other animals. We forget that, in evolutionary terms, we are a very new species, and that the more animalistic, primitive structures in the brain are very much at play in daily life. The image that stares back at us in the mirror is a product of the delicate relationship between those powerful, raw urges and our higher "human" functions.

The brain's higher cortical functions are connected to older structures that evolved to become richly associated with a person's sense of "self." The amygdala, for instance, located in the brain's limbic region and involved in the regulation of emotions and moods, connects to the frontal lobes via the upper portions of the temporal lobe. So does the hippocampus, a limbic center for memory and imagery. This is why a person's "feeling" of selfhood can be such a highly exhilarating experience, and also why concerns about self-preservation can be so infused with fear.

One strategy to protect the self, scholars of evolution inform us, is to find a common ground for cooperation; the other is to attack and destroy one's enemies. Our brain is equipped with powerful machinery to direct both forms of behavior. Fortunately, its higher centers have the potential to inhibit more primitive limbic urges, thus enhancing the odds of group survival.

According to ethologist Frans de Waal, survival of a wide range of species, including humans, has often involved a process of sharing and reciprocation. Without this "enlightenment and self-interest," the survival of early human groups would have been impossible. In *Good Natured*, de Waal emphasizes that social groups set up systems of checks and balances to delay immediate gratification and to reinforce cooperative living. Primates, for example, show great sympathy for injured individuals; food sharing is also common.

Anthropologist Robin Fox contends, in *The Challenge of Anthropology*, that cultures must work hard to maintain cooperation. It requires the inhibition of primitive urges through "initiation, intimidation, sublimation, bribery, education, work and superstition." For, beneath the cooperative surface, there is a steady drumbeat of individual desires seeking expression. An escalation of tensions can happen very rapidly: someone provokes an emotion in us; we become angry; stress builds; adrenaline is released; there is more tension; breathing rate increases; heartbeat accelerates; blood pressure rises; finally, there is a move either to fight or to de-escalate. Because our higher brain functions enable us to anticipate the consequences of actions, we can usually avoid physical battle. Instead, we run from potentially violent encounters; we spit out harsh words and then back off; we become sullen or depressed, or plan revenge; or we divert our aggression to the basketball court.

Or we fantasize. On August 20, 1992, *The Mirror*, a popular Montreal weekly entertainment newspaper, published a spirited column that vented some highly charged violent fantasies. The author, Julianne Pidduck, explained that she was tired of being harassed by men when out for a walk with her dog; she was also generally infuriated about rape, child abuse and wife battering. Her fantasies included "forming a squadron of tough mamas armed to the hilt and when something's going down, we move in and rough up the offenders a bit . . . maybe brand them with a big 'O' (for offensive to women) between the eyes for future identification." And, she added, "if they're real assholes, there's the Thelma and Louise solution"—blowing them away, as featured in the film about two women who reach their limit of tolerance of abusive men.

The column caused two college professors to protest to the local press council that Pidduck was inciting mass murder of men and promoting hatred against males as a group. (The public reaction to their protest was dismissive contempt and laughter.) Pidduck gave voice to thoughts and images of many women who feel vulnerable to male violence. Those professing to be shocked that a woman could have such fantasies are not being fully honest. We all have fantasies: Getting our revenge on the boss. Punching out the local bully. Shooting out the tires of a tail-gater. Torturing a sadistic killer.

Violent fantasies, verbal threats and menacing body language are all examples of the "rumblings" that both infuse society with much of its tensions and often defuse outright battle. Fox finds similarities between these human behaviors and ritualizations in primates—displays such as baring teeth and menacing movements. "If things get too hot," he writes, "the animal can withdraw and flee. It can submit and show deference. As ethologists have demonstrated in species after species, the vast majority of fighting stops at the ritual level."

In both primate and human societies, however, opportunities for conflict invariably result, at some point, in expressions of violence. De Waal views violence in our culture as "an inevitable phase in relations among individuals." Fox adds that, "if we are constantly presented with situations in which violence seems to be the only solution, then we will resort to it with a measure of courage, sadness, dignity, grim determination, cool efficiency, religious devotion and sheer insane glee."

The research of Michael Persinger at Laurentian University in Sudbury, Ontario, dramatizes how the belief systems many people consider a powerful antidote to everyday violence may indeed actually facilitate violence. It has to do with how the "self" is constructed, and how inhibitions to violence can be removed. A strong summation of the theoretical foundations of some of this work can be found in Persinger's 1987 book, *Neuropsychological Bases of God Beliefs*.

Like Nobel laureate Francis Crick, the co-discoverer of the structure of DNA now involved in brain science, Persinger is questioning the basis of religious experience. Working with both healthy men and women and those who have experienced brain trauma, Persinger has been able to reproduce mystical and paranormal experiences, including perceptions of being visited by gods, demons or other apparitions, and even of being abducted by alien creatures. People have long reported being inspired by muses, visited by angels, sexually manipulated by incubi and succubi, and even spoken to by God. Persinger has experimental evidence from about 600 subjects that he can stimulate such experiences by stimulating regions of the brain electromagnetically.

The subject sits blindfolded on a comfortable chair alone in a sound-proof chamber; he or she wears a motorcycle helmet outfitted with electrodes. The lights are turned off and the door is closed. For about twenty minutes, selected portions of the subject's brain receive irregular pulses of an electromagnetic field controlled by computer. Some individuals get such a strong sense of "presence" in the room that they feel their bodies being grabbed or manipulated. Others experience strongly positive but less precise feelings of presence.

Persinger's uncompromising hypothesis that religious and mystical experiences are brain constructs which can be simulated in a laboratory is not a small claim in a world in which most individuals believe, often aggressively, in a god. For Persinger, mystical encounters are "the kernels around which religious beliefs and convictions have emerged." As cultures around the world reinforce these experiences as real events, we consider them to be normal. The cold reality, he says, is that "there is not one iota of empirical evidence that they're real."

In a 1983 paper, Persinger posed a provocative question: Could a certain type of microseizure drive a person "to kill with the conviction of cosmic consent"? Over the years, his research has suggested that the answer is yes: this phenomenon can build up to the point where someone kills in the name of God. There are, of course, countless historical examples.

It continues to concern the empiricist in Persinger that the God paradigm exerts such control over society, that people may kill others or sacrifice themselves in defending their deity. Moreover, he says, the temporal-lobe structures that produce the God experience are the very same as those associated with aggression. Thus, the temporal lobe plays an important role in both ecstatic experience and violent behavior.

Persinger believes God experiences are particularly dangerous in light of the threat of nuclear nightmare. "Who would you rather have with his finger on the button?" he asks. "A person who realizes that experiences are neurological? Or someone who believes in an afterlife?"

Persinger's theories about the brain employ knowledge about electrical activity in the brain and the nature of seizures, linkages between the two hemispheres, and the workings of the temporal lobe. Studies have shown that structures strongly associated with the regulation of emotional life, such as the limbic region's amygdala, are highly unstable electrically. Studies have also shown that, when the amygdala and hippocampus are stimulated in humans during surgery, patients report perceptions of strange beings and mystical encounters.

But how do such perceptions occur in everyday life? Persinger believes that subtle forms of microseizures in the right or left temporal lobe—neuron firings imperceptible to the individual—cause a brief disturbance in the normal processing of information in the brain. This changes the way information flows from one brain hemisphere to the other. Normally, the two hemispheres are prevented from interfering and competing with each other by neurons in the cortex that send information across the band of fibers of the corpus callosum. Persinger proposes that a microseizure temporarily disables this safety feature. When this occurs, a person's sense of self, which emerges largely from language functions regulated by the brain's left hemisphere, is suddenly altered. Persinger theorizes that the right hemisphere's sense of self briefly intrudes on the left side and creates an altered state or the feeling of another "self" or "presence."

Persinger believes this self tends to be murky because the right hemisphere is dominant for non-verbal, spatial tasks, and usually is unsophisticated in language. Therefore, experiences filtered by the right hemisphere would likely reflect distortions of visual and spatial patterns, accompanied by great personal emotion. This, says Persinger, would explain why some people report what look like demons, odd-shaped humanoids or poorly organized human body forms.

Persinger's confidence in his theory grew as he studied individuals who had suffered damage to the corpus callosum. In one study of fifty patients, a thorough neuropsychological examination revealed that 62 percent of them reported otherworldly experiences. Tests also showed that the patients were unusually prone to having temporal-lobe microseizures.

Many people with brain injuries think they are going crazy because they begin to feel that they are "not the same person." Some experience a sense of presence, and a sense that these spirits wish to claim them. One patient experienced a God-like presence sitting by the left side of her body most nights for about thirty minutes just before she fell asleep.

But the shearing of the corpus callosum is not the only cause of such effects. Persinger says anyone has the potential to experience them if microseizures cause above-normal electrical activity in the right hemisphere as compared with the left. Triggers include fatigue, stress, a mild reduction of oxygen in cells, the use of psychoactive drugs, surgery, and even a shift in one's sleeping schedule. Some individuals, however, may be more vulnerable to these shifts of "self" because they have greater electrical instability within their amygdala and hippocampus.

Persinger has provided a plausible theory of how the "self" can change in response to processes deep in the brain stimulated by environmental inputs. He makes it more difficult for us to look at ourselves in the mirror and assess that we have "self-control" over what we see and feel.

One exposure in Persinger's sound-proof chamber to a computer-delivered dose of electromagnetic waves makes one aware of the fragility of one's "self" and how that sense of self can be altered, at least temporarily. I know—I did the test. I didn't see "God," but I became directly involved with a stream of faces bursting out at me and quickly flying into what seemed like a starlit night. Some seemed clownish. Others appeared to be demonlike and looking for a fight. All seemed as real as any character I might meet during the day.

I told Persinger that the experience was at times mildly frightening but mostly pleasant, even intoxicating. "I gave you a pretty mild stimulation of the temporal lobe because we want to treat our guests well," he said. "Maybe we'll do more the next time."

It's worth noting that Persinger's theories and experiments have provoked some devout servants of God to threaten his life.

II

We begin life with a biological legacy ready to be fine-tuned by culture. We are born with billions of brain cells that require connections so learning will occur. The neurons that are stimulated into action create very different brain anatomies, which can be reconfigured through ongoing changes in experience. Those neurons not used will die off.

To function well, the brain must be well exercised early in life; otherwise, intellectual growth will be impeded. A report by the Carnegie Corporation, which devotes considerable time and money to studying early development, emphasizes the dangers of inadequate early brain stimulation. For example, children born into impoverished environments can show signs of learning problems by eighteen months of age; some may be irreversible, and some, it is often reasoned, may make it more difficult to inhibit violent actions. Research at the University of Montreal suggests that, if children are not taught to inhibit "natural" aggression by age three, they will be inclined to be aggressive.

Old-fashioned sociological and psychological studies suggest that poverty and community influences—family disruption, high population turnover and residential mobility, high density in housing, and few social resources—somehow combine to produce high rates of violent crime. This may be so, but the explanation of why there is so much violence in some economically disadvantaged, disproportionately black communities in the United States must include the way these social factors affect biology. Many American inner cities have epidemic levels of violence. Children grow up in the midst of guns, knives and gang wars. Some 100,000 American children, mostly in poor neighborhoods, take guns to school every day. (Many schools employ metal detectors and conduct locker sweeps to reduce the gunplay.) These same children see people die from gun blasts, drive-by shootings and stabbings. This exposure to powerful environment stressors disrupts early brain development and learning and makes it difficult for children to form close attachments. Studies show a strong correlation between living with these circumstances and the likelihood of becoming violent.

Some sociologists look at violence in the inner city as a result of economic deprivation. In *When Work Disappears*, William Julius Wilson emphasizes that huge job losses devastated the inner cities of the United States between 1967 and 1976. (For example, 1 million manufacturing jobs were lost in Chicago, New York, Philadelphia and Detroit.) Unemployment among blue-collar blacks rose dramatically in the 1970s and early 1980s. At this time, too, the black middle class moved out of the inner cities, removing, Wilson believes, what might have been a buffer against the social consequences of joblessness.

According to sociologist Elijah Anderson, what filled the gap in the inner-city neighborhoods was an "oppositional culture," a culture of the streets for those with no faith in mainstream rules. In such a culture, self-esteem depends on control of turf and commodities, including drugs, and a gun blast is a fitting response to someone who doesn't show due respect.

What is not usually explored is the likely evolutionary component of this turn to violence, which can be an adaptive response for economic and personal survival. Survival in this environment often means using a gun. Inhibition of the need to protect the "self" can mean death.

The "oppositional culture" described by Anderson is by no means a new phenomenon. It has its historical roots in inequality, oppression and racism both in the United States and elsewhere. It is the sad product of a world divided into haves and have-nots, a world reinforcing the social conditions that breed daily conflict and violence. And it foretells two possible futures: one in which conflict, not cooperation, will rule; or one in which the mighty will maintain social order by subduing any challenges to its conventions.

III

Because our culture encourages the belief that aggressive behavior can be inhibited by an act of the will, it can be extremely difficult for people to comprehend what appears to be an "eruption" of extreme or unusual violence.

On April 2, 1994, in Montreal, three boys, aged thirteen, fourteen and fifteen, beat an elderly couple to death. When they were arrested, two of the boys were defiant, even giving the finger to the TV cameras.

The community, pumped up by high-profile coverage in the media, reacted angrily to the brutality, but there was also considerable shock and confusion: how could young boys commit such horrible, senseless killings?

There was a similar reaction to the murder of a fifty-five-year-old in Atlanta. The man, crippled by multiple sclerosis, was attacked for many hours. He was stabbed with a kitchen knife and a barbecue fork, strangled with a rope, and hit on the head with a hammer and the barrel of a shotgun. Three males, aged twenty-four, seventeen and fifteen, were promptly arrested.

The fact is that these violent acts rarely "erupt." Boys or young adults who commit them do not suddenly turn into killers. They are often verbally and physically abused or neglected in early childhood and have trouble learning social norms in school. They become cold, hardened, detached, lacking the ability to empathize and inhibit violent feelings. Their psychiatric assessments often conclude that there is little hope for rehabilitation; that, as adults, they will likely commit other acts of violence. Thus, there is evidence to suggest that these violent events may be the result of a steady process of disinhibition that heightens the probability of violence.

In adulthood, as in childhood, inhibitions can be gradually broken down until the "self" changes sufficiently to reach a breaking point. An event or a series of events can finally push an individual over the edge.

The film *Falling Down* is a story about the destruction of "the American Dream." What it perhaps inadvertently provides is an example of what might happen when the veils of self-control are slowly removed until the individual reaches a threshold or "breaking point" at which the brain's inhibitions to violence are overwhelmed.

The story line is simple. A man has lost his job. He has split up with his wife and misses his daughter. We first see him in a traffic snarl in Los Angeles. Agitated, he leaves his car and heads on foot to his former home, hoping to arrive in time for his daughter's birthday party.

On the way, he drops in to purchase something in a convenience store, which he nearly destroys, after rightly accusing the owner of charging exorbitant prices.

He is next harassed by two gang members; he cracks one of them with a baseball bat. Several gang members then come after him with semi-automatic weapons, but he escapes, watches their car crash and takes their weapons.

He then terrorizes a crowded fast-food restaurant after the waitress insists it's too late to serve him breakfast; kills the owner of a Nazi memorabilia store, who insinuates that they are birds of a feather; and causes a wealthy golfer to have a heart attack by brandishing his weapons after the golfer reacts negatively to his presence on the exclusive course.

He tracks his wife and daughter to an ocean pier. There, a cop persuades him to stop the violence. Before killing himself, the man appears confused and asks the cop: "Am I the bad guy?"

The movie suggests that crossing the line into violence can be the consequence of a collapsing life—serious marital problems, the loss of a job, few remaining friends and an inability to cope with the failure. But the same smoldering, slow build-up to murder also appears in the American workplace. Each year, about 1,000 people are killed on the job, a rise of about 30 percent since the 1980s. One workplace survey in the United States conducted by a major insurance company suggests that more than 2 million employees suffer physical attacks each year, and more than 6 million are threatened.

The workplace is hierarchically structured, often with rigid rules of conduct. Managers can exert strong control over employees, leaving them with little dignity and sense of worth. To keep their jobs, people have always put up with abuse—intimidation, verbal abuse and sexual harassment. Resentments are certain to build up over time toward bosses and highly competitive, mean-spirited or merely successful co-workers.

At what point do the rumblings lead to conflict, and then violence? While the exact point varies with the individual, disinhibition caused by the lack of social supports is usually the culprit. Men who are loners are most likely to kill on the job. Women, who generally have more social supports, rarely kill a co-worker.

The gradual rise of tensions and disinhibition leading to violence also occurs with child abuse. Each year in the United States, parents or close relatives kill about 1,300 children, two-thirds of them younger than ten years of age. Studies show that these murders are typically the culmination of bullying, threats, intimidation, kicks, slaps, punches and beatings. (About 160,000 American children are harmed each year, according to government statistics. This is probably a considerable underestimate: not only is there underreporting, but many people, particularly the poor, are ignored for survey purposes.)

The 3,000 American men who kill their female partners each year also often gradually build up to the act as they discard inhibitions. Some of the most violent and dangerous husbands show little impulsiveness; indeed, their assaults tend to be well calculated to instill fear. They actually become calmer during the beatings; even their heart rates drop.

Many of the 4 million American men who annually cause harm to wives and girlfriends are between the ages of eighteen and thirty and are often under great stress. They tend either to be unemployed or to hold poorly paid jobs. Many domestic battles center on increasing male possessiveness and the need to control the relationship. Men frequently explain their violence in terms of fearing abandonment or rejection; many have learned from their fathers that physical violence keeps wives in line. They are also likely to use drugs or retreat into binge drinking. ("Crack" cocaine, for example, can lead to psychotic states, and it is likely, as new research suggests, that cocaine's rapid access to the brain distorts brain signals. It is thought that the alcohol–violence link involves complex brain processes that can be influenced by cultural rules of conduct.)

Another factor often found in the profile of the wife batterer is evidence of head injury. A study of batterers conducted at the University of Massachusetts Medical School found such evidence in the majority of the men who participated. A head injury appears to affect cortical functions that are important in controlling aggressive impulses.

Not all of the factors mentioned above that can cause disinhibition and predispose individuals to violence have had the attention they deserve, in part as a result of gross neglect of wife battery in our culture. (The high-profile U.S. National Commission on the Causes and Prevention of Violence did not even mention it in its 1970 report on violent crime.)

Research in the past fifteen years has gradually revealed that wife battery is a widespread norm: in a lifetime, one-fifth to one-third of all women will suffer some physical abuse from a partner or ex-partner.

Studies indicate that women seek hospital emergency help for battering—concussions, broken bones, damage to joints, loss of hearing or vision, and burns or knife wounds—more than for any medical reason. Physically abused women typically experience chronic headaches, abdominal pains and muscle aches; recurrent vaginal infections; sleep and eating disorders; and depression.

U.S. national surveys and clinical data indicate that physical abuse occurs during at least 8 percent of pregnancies; the likelihood of assault is slightly greater in months five through nine. The consequences sometimes include fetal fractures; rupture of the uterus, liver and spleen; and premature delivery.

Many women who are assaulted regularly are also raped regularly by their mates. Between one-third and one-half of women who have been physically abused say they have also been raped by their partners. These women experience many of the reactions to rape—depression, self-loathing, suicidal urges—that women who are raped by strangers undergo.

The focus on the physical abuse of women intensified during and after the extensive coverage of the criminal and civil trials of O.J. Simpson, related to the slaying of his ex-wife, Nicole Brown Simpson, and Ronald Goldman on June 12, 1994. Reports that Simpson had physically abused his wife aroused indignation and sparked media special reports about wife battering. The number of calls by abused women to emergency hot lines increased dramatically after Simpson's arrest.

Our culture, however, still focuses on only part of the explanation of why men batter women. Feminist theory, for example, holds that a patriarchal society rewards female submissiveness and male dominance and aggression: boys are taught to raise their voices and be tough; girls are encouraged to be quiet and seek (male) help. First the family, and then male-dominated community institutions, reinforce these values.

That's an important part of the story of violence; but biology, too, plays a part. There continues to be strong resistance to acknowledging that social forces and alteration of brain functions can release inhibitions, resulting in violence. We also neglect the evolutionary component in day-to-day violence—namely, that violence is an overwhelmingly male activity in every culture and that the abuse of women is pervasive. For example, in Brazil, wife battering is so common that special police stations have been created to deal with the problem. In India, many women die in fires started by husbands or relatives who hope to acquire a better dowry from the next marriage. In Bombay, one of every four deaths of women aged fifteen to twenty-four is the consequence of such "accidents": their clothes catch fire and they burn to death.

All in all, we should focus on how difficult it can be—and how much harder we shall have to try—to inhibit socially the powerful, age-old forces of violence.

This suggestion, however, would not necessarily please proponents of the view that women can be just as violent as men. Katherine Dunn, writing in *Mother Jones*, proposes that women have always fiercely protected themselves and their offspring, and this ability remains; society, however, has assigned men the right to violence and women a place in "the halls of peace and passivity." True, if somewhat overstated, but Dunn then leaps to claim that some research shows that women contribute as much as men to domestic violence. (Some male-advocacy groups have also suggested as much.) The only credible available data, however, suggest that, while women may start fights as often as men, men more often commit multiple acts of violence during a fight, cause more injury and kill more often.

What wife batterers, workplace killers, child abusers and killers, and children who kill have in common is this: all reach a breaking point after living with warning symptoms that have escalated, usually gradually. Most of these individuals do not appear unusual; nor could their behavior much of the time foretell that they would commit horrible acts of violence. On any given day, they would appear to be "us." They only become "them" when they separate from the human pack *temporarily* to strike with cold-bloodedness or fury.

IV

Given our evolutionary capacity for violence, the powerful environmental stimuli that we process and our self-preoccupation, we should
expect that our world would be violent. Perhaps it is striking that
there isn't *more* violence.

Year in and year out, official North American homicide rates
remain fairly stable, as do rates for other forms of violent crime. The
occasional upswings and downswings are believed to reflect different
patterns in law enforcement and shifting demographics.

It is not violence but fear that is on the increase, perhaps because
of heightened attention to extreme and random violence.

To reduce violence significantly over the long term would require
extraordinary shifts in everyday learning and belief systems, major
changes in those aspects of the everyday environment that foster violence, and considerable alteration of the flow and registration of information in the brain.

We would do better to consider that current levels of violence are
as *mild* as they are likely to get.

5

The "Rape Culture":

Where Fantasy Ends and Violence Begins

I

Over the years, a notable effort has been expended in trying to clarify the sex–violence connection. Considering the variations of sexual aggression—from sexual threats to rape and murder—it's disquieting to find that the explanations that have dominated public attention do little genuine explaining, but fit neatly into transparent agendas. Among them are the feminist position that male domination of society is responsible for most sexual violence, and the religious preoccupation with sexuality as something "evil."

Our culture has ignored the accumulating scientific evidence that social factors and human biology combine to unleash violence, including sexual violence. The brain, as the organ of behavior, processes cultural inputs—including sexual and violent imagery and messages. The primitive structures in the brain's limbic region are thought to be involved in the expression of rage and sexual desire, while cortical structures are key to a system of checks. When this system of inhibition breaks down, the beast is often turned loose. There is so much sexual violence in our society that some social critics have named our way of life a "rape culture." It is that and more.

❖

In North America, it is estimated that as many as one in eight women will be sexually violated, in some way, in her lifetime. Some rapes will cause serious injuries, disfigurement, and even death; more often, the results will be genital injury, laceration and abrasions. Most of the time, the damage will be primarily psychological.

Feminist theory argues that sexual violence is typical of a patriarchal social structure, which depends upon the oppression and control of women. This perspective sheds some light on violent behavior, but is not comprehensive.

For decades, medical theory has defined rape as "pathological," which presupposes a non-existent baseline for "normalcy." Feminists rail against this view of rape, with good reason. For viewing rape as a *disease* neglects the role of culture. Historically, medicine has explained rape in terms of hypothetical—and irresistible—impulses buried deep in the psyche. As expert witnesses, psychiatrists trotted out the impulse theory time and again in the courts, depicting rapists as victims of overpowering impulses, who had no idea what they were doing when they raped.

Feminists retorted that rapists knew full well what they were doing, and were responsible for their actions. No way were men going to be absolved of the responsibility for rape.

Sociologist Diana Scully's 1990 report on rape, *Understanding Sexual Violence*, was heralded by many as an antidote to psychiatric foolishness. After interviewing 114 convicted rapists and 75 other inmates, she concluded that, by and large, men rape because they are encouraged to do so by a society that rewards men for violence against women. For some men, she states, "rape is a low-risk, high-reward act." Though Scully believes there are some rapists who are undoubtedly "mentally ill," she views most rapes as deliberate, methodical acts to attain revenge, access to unwilling women, power or adventure. Our rape culture can be neutralized, Scully insists, only if "men are forced to admit that sexual violence is *their* problem."

Scully's findings tell us what rapists say they do and why they think they do it. However, while her report yields some insights into the ways a patriarchal system excuses rape, it doesn't tell us much about how the desire for rape is aroused and takes shape.

Feminists have rightly argued that the psychiatric "ownership" of sexual violence has limited our understanding of it, but the same can be said about feminist studies that exclude biology. We need more than apparent truth-telling by convicted rapists to explain the complexities of human behavior. We need also to consider clues provided by both brain science and the social sciences with regard to the extraordinary power that culture exerts on very malleable brains.

To proclaim that patriarchy is a social construction that preserves itself only through social reinforcement doesn't jibe with what we are learning about the biological and psychosocial complexities of being human.

Not all feminist theory ignores biology. Back in 1970, Shulamith Firestone wrote, in *The Dialectic of Sex*, that women need to seize control of reproduction in order to free themselves from male tyranny. Firestone believed that nature can be thwarted by eliminating pregnancy and substituting artificial reproduction. Feminists such as Betty Friedan, who espouse a reverence for child-bearing and the concept of biological division, Firestone argued, were ensuring the inevitable control of females by males, in the family unit and beyond.

Other feminists have come to an accommodation with the contributions of biology to learning. For example, sociologist Alice Rossi argued in the 1960s that men and women, though physiologically different, would be very much alike socially if social barriers to women were brought down. By 1977, she had reluctantly (and bravely) changed her opinion, writing in the journal *Daedalus* that men and women differed *biologically* in their parenting abilities. She no longer believed that family patterns could be explained solely by the social engineering of patriarchy. Women dominate child care in all societies. Why? Because the female is more involved in reproduction and nurture than is the male.

In her 1984 presidential talk to the American Sociological Association, Rossi explained that male–female diversity "emerged from the long prehistory of mammalian and primate evolution." To tiptoe around this, she warned, would lead sociology to risk "eventual irrelevance."

Rossi, in focusing on parenting, opened up a Pandora's box for feminist theory. If there were differences in parenting, why not in other realms of behavior, including sexual violence? For example, evolutionary psychologists (who sometimes call themselves "sociobiologists") suggest that rape is evolution's way of enabling males to gain access to otherwise unavailable females. When cultural patterns of sexuality stand in the way of an individual male's sexual fulfillment, rape becomes a way of influencing natural selection. It's perhaps best to view this as an obsolete or maladaptive ancient pattern that no longer has any survival value.

Yet, as we search for an understanding of sexual violence, we must begin with the premise that humans have a brain with complex structures which tie us to a more primitive, evolutionary past. And we can further investigate the proposition—such work has been done in both animal and human studies—that some of these structures, located in the deeper parts of the brain, are capable of directing both violence and powerful sexual feelings.

The link between the sudden onset of sexually violent behavior and a rapid breakdown of inhibitions is particularly evident when men go to war. They not only fight: some also rape, often with the tacit or explicit permission of those "in command."

Feminist Phyllis Chesler, writing of the war in Bosnia, provides accounts of the extreme sexual violence that occurred when the usual societal norms were suspended; how Serbian, Croat and Moslem soldiers broke into homes, beat women, and gang-raped them and their daughters. She sums up: "Male soldiers treated female civilians the way 'kinky johns' treat whores, the way psychotic wife batterers treat their wives." Chesler, however, apparently sees this behavior as a feature of how Balkan men view women and sex: "Perhaps this is what some men think is 'manly' in the Balkans."

The fact is, anywhere war has raged, men have raped women. Therefore, not to search out the role biology plays in these barbarous assaults doesn't make sense.

All too often, any consideration of biology is tossed out as conservative thinking that offers no hope for change. Feminists who see patriarchy as the overarching cause of sexual violence against women treat biology as an apologia for the supporters (mainly male) of the status quo. However, as Rossi put it in 1984, "ignorance of biological processes may doom efforts at social change to failure because we misidentify what the targets for change should be, and hence what our means should be to attain the change we desire."

The rape culture has its extreme behaviors, and they too can be viewed as products of the interplay between cultural inputs and the brain's potential for triggering violence.

The fusion of sexual urges and violence can produce savagery. Some men terrorize and torture their female victims, kill them, butcher them, and then violate their body parts. Sometimes they carve out the genitals, and even eat them. Such men derive sexual pleasure not only by controlling and injuring women, but also from the victim's fear and pain.

Studies have shown that sexual sadists tend to be quiet, introspective, studious, mild-mannered and very polite. They are tidy in their personal appearance, even timid. They also tend to be sexual prudes. Most who admit to committing violent acts appear not to identify strongly with either sex. Some will show longings for the feminine, including signs of transvestism; in rare cases, there is a desire for a sex change. The sexual sadist will most likely attack after suffering injury to his self-esteem.

What can we make of this sexual fury? As sexual sadism represents a tiny extreme of male sexual violence toward women, it hasn't received much research attention. Controlled studies are few; what is known is culled largely from psychological profiles of convicted sadists and from neurophysiological tests and brain scans.

Some of the more elaborate research is medically oriented, and has been conducted at the Clarke Institute of Psychiatry in Toronto. The Clarke, which is affiliated with the University of Toronto, has a well-respected forensic-psychiatry unit that is attempting to refine our understanding of the biological component of sexual violence. One key finding by the institute is that sexual sadists' background profiles are much like those of other sexually aggressive men who are not primarily sadists. They share histories of poor parental supervision, unstable family relationships and childhood abuse or neglect. There are also tendencies in both sadists and non-sadists to abuse alcohol or non-medical drugs and to commit non-sexual crimes, such as theft.

There is, however, some evidence of one intriguing difference between the two groups. In a study published in 1987 in the *Annals of Sex Research*, researchers at the Clarke tested fifty-one sexually violent men for signs of brain impairment, comparing them with a control group of non-violent, non-sex offenders. The sexually violent men were first assessed for sexual sadism; twenty-two qualified. Seven of the twenty-two had killed their victims; their average age was twenty-seven.

When neuropsychological tests were given to both groups, the differences in brain-scan results stood out. Signs of subtle abnormalities in the brain's right temporal lobe were detected significantly more often in sadists than in either non-sadists or controls.

What does this mean? In other studies, damage to the temporal lobe has been linked to both reduced and increased sex drive, and to unusual sexual expression ("anomalies," in psychiatric parlance). One study of temporal-lobe epileptics estimated that close to 20 percent exhibited a sexual anomaly such as sexual compulsion—what we would call a "fetish." Research as far back as the 1960s by then Harvard psychiatrist Frank Ervin and neurosurgeon Vernon Mark revealed a strong association between temporal-lobe epilepsy and violent outbursts (see Chapter 2).

The researchers at the Clarke, citing some of these studies, cautiously concluded that their findings lend support to the theory that "some types of sexual anomalies are associated with subtle forms of brain damage."

A related body of research aimed at "psychopaths"—individuals who commit violent crimes but are considered to be capable of thinking through the consequences of their actions without feelings of guilt—is showing that clues to their behavior may lie in the brain. A common estimate is that about 1 percent of the general population is "psychopathic," as is perhaps as much as 20 percent of the prison population.

One 1991 report by psychologist Robert Hare and his colleagues at the University of British Columbia indicated that in psychopaths there appears to be less than normal use of brain regions that integrate emotions and memory with other brain functions. The researchers reached their conclusion by comparing brain waves of subjects deemed to be psychopaths (on the basis of a questionnaire) with the brain waves of so-called normals. The data were gathered during the performance of a language test that required responses to neutral and emotionally laden words. Research elsewhere with brain scans has since shown that, when psychopaths responded to the emotional words, parts of their brain, such as those regulating emotions (the amygdala) and long-term planning (a region of the frontal cortex), remained inactive; these brain regions in normals were active when they responded to the same words.

The message arising out of this still-preliminary biological research is that a possible defect in the brain's processing of information may make a huge difference in the way some individuals deal with violent urges. Hare and others hope that eventually the biological basis of psychopathy can be pinpointed so that an effective treatment may be developed.

This is certainly possible, but this research is focused largely on extreme forms of violent or sexually violent behavior. As such, it may appear to separate "them" from "us." Given the extent and variations of sexual violence in our culture, this is unsatisfactory.

By common estimate, half a million children are sexually abused each year in the United States. Assume that a number half that large is accurate and it is still overwhelming. Fathers force their young children to have intercourse or oral sex; mothers manipulate their offspring's genitals; uncles rape their nieces and nephews; brothers overpower their siblings; and baby-sitters (female and male) initiate sex play with their charges, often just out of curiosity.

Available statistics and crime reports indicate that it is mostly men who sexually assault children; but, because women are not as forceful in their sexual-abuse patterns and are more likely to abuse children inside the family, more of their assaults may go unreported. It is noteworthy that many male sex offenders claim they were abused by their mother or another female.

The majority of child sex abuse involves family members, relatives and friends—not some stranger on a rampage. The younger the child, the more likely that a family member is the attacker. Yet, it is the stranger who molests children who draws headlines, witchhunts, out-pourings of community fears, and psychiatric interest.

"Pedophilia" is the psychiatric term reserved for individuals who are sexually preoccupied with young children. (Such a preference in males, for example, can be reliably demonstrated; a common test monitors for signs that a penis is becoming erect in subjects watching films of children.)

The brain scans and other tests of male pedophiles, like those of sexual sadists, appear to show significantly more brain abnormality than is found in non-violent, non-sex offenders. A study at the Clarke of forty-one heterosexual, homosexual and bisexual pedophilic out-patients found this abnormality to be typically present in the left temporal and parietal lobes. (The authors of the report carefully note, however, that it is possible for one brain area to compensate for an injured one, especially early in life.) Research on larger groups of pedophiles and more sophisticated scanning technology are needed in order to improve our understanding of the relationship between brain damage and sexual assault on children.

Pedophilia appears to be a deeply entrenched behavioral pattern, and one very resistant to change—even though many pedophiles express remorse and a desire to change. Treatment efforts, such as electric shock and behavioral modification to decondition sexual arousal to children, have produced mixed results. (The administration of electric shock has been banned in some U.S. states.) Castration and the use of a drug such as Depo Provera to lower the testosterone level, and thus reduce sex drive, have not been sufficiently studied to justify their use, although recently passed California legislation will require repeat offenders to receive one of these treatments as a con-dition of parole. (Some critics have called the law a desperate act that ignores scientific evidence. They also call it "barbaric," recalling the

era of the eugenicists in the United States, when so-called undesirables were often sterilized.)

Some pedophiles, however, who find it hard to stop abusing children, ask to be castrated. One fifty-nine-year-old British man with
a long history of sexually assaulting children went on a hunger strike
to pressure authorities to operate on him. In desperation, he had
attempted the deed himself. So did one thirty-two-year-old American
man who claims to have molested 240 children. Calling himself a
"monster" and "demon," he told prison authorities that, without castration, he would continue to rape, and even murder his victims, upon
his release from prison.

This individual likely lives with uncontrollable urges. But what difference is there between child molesters who stalk strangers in school-
yards, and fathers and uncles who regularly rape their young family
members? There are insufficient cultural and biological data to provide
a solid answer, but it has been thought that there are likely to be differences in socialization, and perhaps in brain function. These differences, however, are not likely as significant as we wish to believe.

Meanwhile, some members of communities who rise up in protest
whenever a convicted child molester leaves prison to settle in their
midst might find it instructive to look more closely at what is going
on inside their own homes.

II

In the extreme, sexual violence is obvious; but what some people regard
as harmless behavior others would call violent. To some, a threat, a
look, or verbal pressure might qualify as violence. Others might feel
threats or mild physical persuasion were acceptable behavior, and that
only the physical overpowering of a victim constituted "real" violence.

Feminist theorists rightly contend that a male-dominated society,
with its male-oriented legal system, will often entertain a lot of sexual coercion before calling it violence.

Until about twenty-five years ago, U.S. courts demanded corrobo-
ration of the victim's evidence of the assault. This requirement kept rape

trials to a minimum. Though there has been considerable change in the statutes, the courts are having a difficult time deciding how much force is necessary in an incident in order to convict for rape or sexual assault. In May 1994, the Pennsylvania Supreme Court decided that a woman who repeatedly said "no," but did not resist, was not raped. That same week the California Supreme Court ruled that a rape conviction was allowable even though the woman didn't struggle. In Wisconsin, a man can be found guilty of rape if the woman doesn't agree in advance to sex, and even if she remains silent throughout the act.

Some feminists would like the definition of "rape" extended to situations of verbal coercion, such as may occur on dates. In suggesting that rape is expressed through spoken as well as physical coercion, feminists are acknowledging a continuum of sexual behavior that begins in thought and extends to extreme violence.

Does rape, then, begin with fantasy (defined sometimes as "imagination") fed by everyday imagery, including a wide array of sexual messages? The child molester will often be obsessed with images of children—in pictures, books, videos, even on cereal boxes—and the resulting fantasies will eventually overpower learned inhibitions.

But sexual arousal can occur in almost anyone who is shown sexual images. A study monitoring physiological response to sex films at the University of Amsterdam shows that men and women have the same potential for sexual arousal. They respond equally to sexual cues, which suggests that this is likely a biological predisposition. The study, however, suggests that women may be more discriminating about wanting to have sex as a result of reacting to these cues; perhaps a protective evolutionary component is at play here, given that women must think about pregnancy. The researchers also point out that men are more likely to be affected by sexual stimuli because there are many more sexual cues in the environment directed at men.

Most laboratory studies have focused on male sexual arousal. Those that measure volume changes in the penis have found that about 25 percent of male subjects (typically college students) are sexually aroused when they watch a film depicting a man raping a woman. About 55 percent are aroused when the rape victim is shown to become sexually aroused. Viewings have led some male subjects to exhibit heightened sexual aggression toward women in the laboratory setting. It also appears that these males are more likely than others to use force in their sexual behavior outside the lab setting.

Sociologists such as Diana Russell believe that portrayals of women as sexual objects to be controlled and manipulated make some men want to rape women and intensify that existing desire in others. This is so because sexual fantasy can undermine inhibitions, wearing down both internal checks on desire and learned precepts regarding certain behaviors.

No one is claiming that the sterile environment of psychological testing is an adequate substitute for observation of the real world, yet the results of these studies are very consistent. And they do make sense. Any male who has ever masturbated with *Playboy* knows that sexual images fuel fantasy, and fantasy often leads to action. How much action and in what form, and how harmful it is to others, is as variable as sexuality itself. Thus, we have sexual sadists, child molesters, fathers who prey on their children, rapists who stalk strangers by night, husbands who force their wives to perform sexual acts against their will, aggressive males who overpower their reluctant girlfriends, and college students who presume that a date automatically means sex.

Many men contend that they couldn't possibly sexually abuse a woman, but, under the right circumstances, perhaps they might.

Consider what occurred in well-to-do Glen Ridge, New Jersey, on March 1, 1989. That day, in a basement, thirteen middle-class, high school athletes watched their peers insert a broom handle, a baseball bat and a dirty stick into the vagina of a seventeen-year-old girl with a mental age of eight. The boys joked about it in school the next day.

Eight of the boys were charged with rape. The defense portrayed the victim as a nympho slut who had orchestrated the event to satisfy her voracious sexual appetite. The lawyers built their defense on the notion that what had occurred was normal fun for a bunch of regular guys for whom a sexual opportunity suddenly materialized.

Not so, responded the jury. It convicted three of the boys of first-degree assault-rape and second-degree conspiracy involving the use of the assault objects. However, the judge seemed moved by the young men, whom he described as "not hardened or vicious" and "not without redeeming values." He sent them to a youth facility and gave them a no-minimum sentence. This meant that they could be set free upon being declared rehabilitated—whatever that meant and however long it took.

In July 1993, a report titled *Gender Equality in the Canadian Justice System*, prepared by federal and provincial officials, concluded, among other things, that advertising presenting women as sexual objects was part of a continuum that ended with sexual violence against women.

The report noted: "Aggression against women occurs on a spectrum of activity which moves from non-specific to specific; from a simple advertisement for automobiles or beer in association with the barely-clad women, to murder. The state of mind of the aggressor is only a question of degree."

Another way of looking at sex in advertising is to see it as the "soft" component of sexual imagery. "Hard" components are images such as those rounded up by British authorities in books and videos:

- young girls and boys being raped anally by adults;
- young girls and boys having sex with each other;
- women hanging by their breasts from meat hooks;
- women being penetrated by a dog, donkey or pig;
- men being raped anally by men;
- men putting out their cigarettes on men or women.

As disturbing as these images are likely to be to most individuals, for some they are erotic and fill a need. Human sexuality is a gentle kiss or a passionate embrace, but it is also whipping buttocks until they bleed and frenzied intercourse with a mutilated corpse. Some individuals buy lace to make a "statement." Others pierce ears, nose, breasts and genitals; decorate skin with tattoos; and sport choke collars. Some couples become aroused by watching videos of sexual intercourse. Others become interested only if one of the participants urinates into the other's mouth. Throughout human history, the expression of the sex drive, originating in our animal past and directed by the brain, has been the subject of curious or obsessive experimentation.

Anthropologist Bernard Arcand of Laval University, in Quebec City, contends that pornography enables humans to explore all the possibilities of sexuality. He also suggests that there are universal constants behind the spectrum of expression. For example, modesty is a cultural staple, which, he says, leads to a desire to breach it. As society becomes more technological, according to Arcand, there is more opportunity to enjoy one's sexual preoccupations. Video has made it possible to reinvent any home as a private peepshow.

Does pornography lead to sexual action? Perhaps it reinforces an individual's specific or unfolding need for sexual satisfaction. Can it enable someone to commit an act of sexual violence? Most likely, in association with other social inputs that break down inhibitions. Science isn't yet clear on the exact role of pornography in this process, but a panel convened by the U.S. National Research Council suggested in a 1993 report on various aspects of violence that violent pornography likely interacts with other individual and social factors.

Pornography means something very different to feminist legal scholars such as Catherine MacKinnon. They contend that pornography itself is a hostile act that causes physical and mental harm to women. Pornography is rape. Therefore, such material, which sexually subordinates and dehumanizes women (or children, men and transsexuals), should be banned.

Both MacKinnon and feminist writer Andrea Dworkin helped develop legal arguments against pornography submitted to Canada's Supreme Court. In 1992, the Court ruled in a case involving the distribution of sexual materials that books, pictures, videotapes and the like "portraying women as a class as objects for sexual exploitation could be banned for [their] negative impact on the individual's sense of self-worth." Although the Canadian Charter of Rights and Freedoms, passed in 1982, grants freedom of thought, belief, opinion and expression, it also states that these freedoms are to be qualified by "such reasonable limits prescribed by law as can be demonstrably justified in a free and democratic society."

The Canadian decision is heralded by MacKinnon, Dworkin and others as a triumph over the terror and harm of pornography. Free-speech advocates, including many feminists, view it as an assault on free speech that may produce little diminution of the sexual violence men commit against women.

MacKinnon is quite correct in considering a violent image to be a form of violence. All too often, people underestimate the power of imagery. Many believe that only the weak-minded and debauchers of children are susceptible.

However, MacKinnon is off the mark in thinking that specific violent images, as represented in what she terms "pornography," can be separated from the complex sexual textures of everyday socialization and its powerful reinforcements. She and Dworkin have called for civil legislation that would allow women to sue porn-purveyors if they can provide evidence that the materials have harmed them.

The strategy to enact laws to control sexual expression ignores biological propensities and the ways they can be triggered. It is not likely to make much of a dent in the wide-ranging forms of sexually violent behavior. MacKinnon and Dworkin might as well sue the entire culture and its primitive antecedents.

Quite simply, our culture is steeped in sexual violence. One way to better understand why it is so prevalent is to face up to the human potential for violence and consider the various complex social conditions that can trigger it—in anyone.

In today's society, however, attention is focused on the most extreme forms of violence, which the media report on in great detail. Cases such as that of Paul Bernardo and Karla Homolka in Canada, involving the abduction and sex slayings of two teens, become big-time news. So do some cases of pedophilia and extreme sexual assault. And so do mass murders and serial killings. They become the focus of talk shows and daily discussion. Our culture is well primed to highlight these events and to reinforce the artificial divide between "them" and "us."

6

Serial Killers and Mass Murderers:

Extreme Forms of Ourselves

I

At this moment, somewhere among us, a man nearing middle age, possibly sitting in his office at work, is fantasizing about a pretty woman, about how he will tear apart her body, and then rape her. The man's urge to carry out this fantasy is building slowly, becoming more compelling each day. Like the last time. And the time before that.

One day he will calmly begin to make his fantasies real. Day after day, he will look for the perfect prey, cruising, stalking, wooing, seducing, springing the trap.

The murder will be highly ritualized. The pretty woman will embody a rejection of long ago, and all his suffering will be exorcised by the kill. The scent of it, the blood of it, the power of it will infuse his brain with relief and joy.

So that the pleasure won't fade too quickly, he will keep a memento of the act: a piece of skin, a chopped-off breast, a head. To cherish, perhaps to violate or consume, so that the triumph remains forever part of him.

But the exhilaration will diminish, and something inside him will die. Like the last time.

Then the serial killer's cycle will begin anew.

Each year, scores of serial killers enter and exit the bizarre and frenzied reality in which hundreds, if not thousands, of women and men die. Because more U.S. murders (about one in four) are unsolved now than two decades ago (about one in ten), police agencies, including the U.S. Federal Bureau of Investigation, suggest that serial killing may be on the rise. Since 1970, more serial killings have been reported than in all of previous U.S. history. Though serial killers are found in most nations, the United States, it appears, produces about 75 percent of the world's total.

These chameleon-like killers, hiding behind their social masks, have come to represent extreme violence. They are the supernatural creatures and monsters of our world. In the towns of ancient Europe, their acts likely contributed to the legends of vampires, ghouls and werewolves.

At this moment, somewhere among us, a man between twenty-five and forty is planning the deaths of many people. For years, he has lived with painful memories of when he was savagely beaten and/or sexually violated by his father or mother. And there are all those failures at school, at work, at love. All these years, the anger inside him has been settling into his consciousness. He has been preoccupied with revenge. He is about to commit mass murder. There are now only minor details to work out.

Unlike the serial killer, the mass murderer, who usually strikes once, in a fury, cannot hide among us. He often displays his mounting frustration and vents his anger in public before he lets loose.

What the serial killer and mass murderer have in common is a deeply troubled history and likely a wounded brain. In our culture, however, both are tagged as "monsters" or as "evil." Their acts are perceived as being so inhuman that it is difficult to view these killers as forms of ourselves that have taken an extreme turn. However, our fascination with news stories, movies and books about these individuals betrays us. We sense—and fear—that we are somehow connected to these killers, that there really is no "them" and "us."

The serial killer is not likely to set off alarm bells as he develops his obsession. Indeed, the capacity to blend in with his surroundings is an asset. Take Arthur Shawcross, who can be quite charming; he was convicted of murdering eleven prostitutes in Rochester, New York, over a period of two years.

Shawcross did not suddenly become a "monster." His history reveals a slow build-up to serial killing—numerous academic and behavioral problems in high school, burglary, arson, the murder of two children, and finally the stalking and murder of prostitutes and mutilation of some of the corpses.

His problems began in childhood. Medical records show he was hospitalized for temporary paralysis of the legs. The official diagnosis was encephalitis, an infectious disease, although tests never confirmed this. New York University psychiatrist Dorothy Lewis, who studies biological and social factors in violence, interviewed Shawcross at length in her role as expert witness for his defense. She concluded that his paralysis resulted from having been sexually abused by his mother.

In one videotaped interview, Shawcross is seated in a chair, eyes closed, apparently asleep. (He was actually hypnotized in an effort to probe his memory for evidence of sexual abuse.)

As the videotape plays, Shawcross suddenly moans and cries out, "No more."

Lewis asks in a soft, baby-talk voice: "What's happening to you, Artie?"

Shawcross replies as a child might: "She put a stick in there, my butt . . . No, no, I can't breathe. Ohhh."

Lewis: "What is she doing now?"

Shawcross: "Oh, she pulled it out, and my stomach feels like it's coming out. Ahhh."

Lewis: "What's happening now, Artie?"

Shawcross: "I'm laying on the floor. I can't move. I can't get up. My stomach hurts. Blood is coming out of my bottom, my fanny. I feel like I'm turned inside out."

In the videotaped interview, Shawcross appears to impersonate his mother, as though she has taken hold of his personality. In this guise, he/she re-creates a stabbing.

Lewis gave expert testimony that Shawcross suffered so much sexual abuse as a child that he developed a multiple personality. While controversial, the concept is generally accepted in psychiatry: in seeking to escape horrible suffering, the abused individual's memory, identity and consciousness become fragmented. Personality alternates, which absorb the experience of the abuse and pain, take the place of an integrated personality. According to Lewis, what occurs is a kind of self-hypnosis.

Labeling Shawcross as a "multiple" who could not be responsible for the murders didn't save him from a conviction. The citizens of Rochester and talk-show hosts poked fun at Lewis's testimony. It was even suggested by a prosecution witness that Lewis's hypnosis of Shawcross was "a performance."

Dr. Lewis, however, also believed that Shawcross was brain-damaged.

He had told her in interviews that he would suddenly feel sweaty and shaky prior to a murder, and he would also see blinding white light. After the murder, he would usually fall asleep and, upon awakening, would have only a vague memory of it. There beside him would be the corpse. When he realized what he had done, he would then try to hide the body. Lewis believed Shawcross was having seizures.

She noted that Shawcross had a history of severe head injuries, including a skull fracture, and suffered extreme headaches; occasionally, he blacked out. In earlier research with juveniles, Lewis had concluded that a combination of head injury and early abuse was a time bomb for violence. In one study, the vast majority of the juvenile subjects who became killers showed signs of brain abnormalities. Some had seizures; others had abnormal brain-wave readings. All had been abused in childhood.

Other serial killers studied by Lewis also had traumatic childhoods, which often included head injuries. One such case was Bobby Joe Long, known as the "Classified Ad Rapist" for his assaults on women who placed ads in newspapers. After a motorcycle accident, he developed an extremely powerful sex drive. He began to masturbate at least five times daily, and his need for intercourse with women escalated—

Lewis believed it uncontrollable—at least in part due to damage to the brain's limbic region. He had also suffered other head injuries.

Lewis's view of killers like Long and Shawcross, however, is that their murderous behavior could not be accounted for by any single factor. Rather, it was likely that a variety of forces meshed to produce a nasty killer.

A psychiatric study of Shawcross by Richard Theodore Krauss, commissioned by the public defender's office and reported by Jack Olsen in *The Misbegotten Son*, bears out Lewis's conclusion. Krauss did a thorough job of reaching his conclusion that Shawcross was "not normal" and "extremely dangerous." Shawcross had a small cyst on his right temporal lobe and produced abnormal brain waves that showed evidence of seizures in the temporal and frontal lobes. Krauss interpreted the seizures to be "something short of temporal-lobe epilepsy" (a condition that 1960s studies had linked to violence), but concluded that Shawcross was a "neurologically damaged individual." These neurological observations were much in line with brain studies of other serial killers, which have revealed significant damage to the brain's limbic system.

Krauss had other findings of note. Lab studies revealed that Shawcross had inherited an extra Y (male) chromosome, making him an XYY male, one of about 2,000 born with this genetic anomaly each year in the United States. (Normally one X [female] and one Y chromosome are inherited. Once thought to be associated with violence— that link was subsequently challenged—the condition is strongly associated with learning disabilities and hyperactivity.)

Shawcross, it seems, also had "pyroluria." This is a rare metabolic condition in which there are larger than usual amounts of a biochemical substance called "cryptopyrrole" in the body. Pyroluria had been associated in clinical tests with nervousness, depression, rages, irritability, problems with stress control and mood swings. The condition has been seen as a marker of psychiatric upset in the body. Krauss concluded that "Mr. Shawcross's medical and psychiatric history well document all the clinical correlates found associated with a cryptopyrrole disorder . . ."

Krauss was not called upon to testify at the trial—he submitted his report after the verdict—as he had been commissioned to consider whether Shawcross could beat the charges against him on the grounds of insanity. To be biologically "not normal" is one thing, Krauss concluded; to be insane is another. He could find no hard evidence that Shawcross was not aware of what he was doing when he killed, and awareness was all that counted.

Because Shawcross seemed so "normal"—the kind of person you could have lunch with and never have a clue that he was dangerous, Lewis says—it was inevitable that he would be portrayed by the prosecution as a methodical, cold-blooded killer who had cleverly twirled the sympathetic Lewis around his little finger.

Perhaps he had fooled her—one has to be wary of being taken in by serial killers. They can be very cool and calculating. Some exhibit extraordinary calm under pressure. Take the case of the late Jeffrey Dahmer, who murdered seventeen young men, had sex with some of the corpses, cut the bodies up and ate some body parts. One of Dahmer's prospective victims had escaped from his enslavement. Dahmer was about to return him to the apartment when they were confronted by two policemen. Dahmer convinced them that he and the boy were having a lovers' quarrel. The boy was clearly drugged and handcuffed, but the police believed Dahmer.

Such coolness under pressure may often result from peculiarities in brain chemistry. Preliminary brain-scan data, for example, suggest that a cold-blooded killer has less than normal chemical activity in the prefrontal cortex, possibly suggesting emotional underarousal. The latest research in brain science suggests that this chemical feature may be part of a constellation of brain anomalies that facilitate murderous behavior. However, not everyone agrees that such is the case with serial killers: The prosecution in the Shawcross case did not. Neither did the jury. Neither did the citizens of Rochester.

Resistance in our culture to acknowledging the biological contributions to serial killing is understandable. The stakes are high, for if we accept the explanation that the behavior of "monsters" in our midst has to do with the firings of neurons, what would that say about our own potential for violence? It is much less threatening to assume that "monsters" are driven by some evil force that they willfully refuse to control.

The other "monsters" in our culture are mass murderers.

On December 6, 1989, at the age of twenty-five, Marc Lepine killed fourteen female engineering students at the University of Montreal's École Polytechnique and injured fifteen other women and men. It is the worst mass murder in Canadian history.

Lepine had no criminal record. He was never a mental patient. But he came to believe that women were asking for too much change, and that enraged him. Feminists needed to be taught a lesson. His killing spree with a legally purchased semi-automatic weapon was a symbolic act against the feminist enemy. And it was worth dying for. Lepine then shot himself.

Lepine's early childhood abuse appears to have laid the foundation for extreme violence. His was a turbulent childhood, including the humiliation and pain of being beaten often by his father and of watching helplessly as his father often beat his mother. As a teenager, Lepine seemed socially backward, unable to mix well with others. Being rejected both by the military and by the University of Montreal's engineering school—the very school that was signing up women—likely helped to push him over the edge. Women, particularly strong-willed women, emerged as *the enemy*.

Revenge is often the driving force in mass murder. This was the case in September 1949, when twenty-eight-year-old Howard Unruh of Camden, New Jersey, went hunting. Some of his neighbors were slandering him, he figured. With 9-mm Luger in hand, and dressed in a brown suit, white shirt and striped bow-tie, he visited the local shoestore, barbershop and drugstore. Over a period of twelve minutes, he shot thirteen people, including children, who happened to be in his path.

Unruh's "revenge" marked the beginning of the modern era of mass murder; unpredictable killings, mostly of strangers, by men who usually had turbulent childhoods, were socially isolated, were obsessed with guns, and over many years had built up both a hatred for individuals or groups and a hunger for revenge. While these characteristics are common among mass murderers, there are numerous variations of deep-rooted unrest. Unruh, for example, was a moody, reclusive target-shooter who built a fence, with a large gate, around the home where he lived with his parents. When the gate was stolen, it was payback time. After being apprehended, he was judged by psychiatrists to be suffering from hallucinations and delusions.

George Hennard also came to hate, particularly his domineering, high-strung mother, whom he saw as having caused him much unhappiness and stress in childhood. He would often refer to her as a "viper" and tended to see most women as such. At noon, on October 16, 1991, Hennard drove his pickup truck through the large plate-glass window of Luby's Cafeteria in Killeen, Texas. He shot dead twenty-two of the customers and wounded twenty-three. Most were women.

Many mass murderers build up slowly to their day of infamy. An FBI report shows that Patrick Purdy was a friendless drifter who did odd jobs and lived in skid-row flophouses. He was arrested on numerous occasions and let go, except for some small-time convictions: between 1979 and 1987, he was run in for extortion and possession of a dangerous weapon; he was caught soliciting sex from a policewoman; he was charged with possession of hashish and marijuana; and he was found with stolen property.

When Purdy was jailed in 1987 for being an accessory to a robbery and for firing a pistol in a national park and resisting arrest, he tried unsuccessfully to cut his wrists with his fingernails and toenails, and then to hang himself. At this point, he was considered by probation experts to be a danger to himself and others, but was set free after spending forty-five days in jail.

On January 17, 1989, Purdy drove his station wagon to the Cleveland Elementary School in Stockton, California, where he had been a student from 1969 to 1973. He wore a camouflage jacket under a flak jacket, and had painted the front of his shirt to read: "Libya, Earthman and PLO." And he had painted its back to read: "Freedom," and "Death to the Great Satin [*sic*]."

Purdy carried a semi-automatic pistol and an AK-47, a semi-automatic rifle. He had bought these guns in Oregon and California, using aliases. In his seedy motel room, he kept a miniature army of tanks, jeeps, weapons and a hundred two-inch soldiers.

Outside the schoolyard, he borrowed from military strategy. He set fire to his station wagon to divert attention from his entry through a back gate to a play area. About 400 children, most aged six to nine, were having recess.

Calm, silent, Purdy opened fire. After killing five children and wounding thirty others, he shot himself dead.

A similar event took place in Dunblane, Scotland, in March 1996, where Thomas Hamilton killed sixteen kindergarten children and wounded twelve others. He also killed one teacher and wounded two. Hamilton, using four handguns, fired haphazardly, first in the schoolyard, and then in the auditorium where the children were having gym class. He then killed himself.

Prior to the killings, Hamilton, a loner with a penchant for photographing young boys, had been writing letters to townspeople and politicians, saying that he had been unfairly ostracized as a pervert. He even wrote to Queen Elizabeth. The letters were smoldering with unresolved tension. In the end, the Dunblane school paid the price.

But while individuals with troubled histories are numerous in our society, relatively few go to the extreme of mass murder. Like Thomas Hamilton, many individuals build up resentments; but most of them do not go on a killing rampage. Like Marc Lepine, many have abusive childhoods; yet most do not declare war on a particular group of people. And most repeat violent offenders stop short of the mass slaughter engaged in by a Patrick Purdy or a Howard Unruh. Why do some explode when others do not?

Brain science, of late, has been offering clues that might help us understand some of the biological dynamics which may interact with such factors as early childhood troubles and stressful environments. Evidence is being gathered that shows that changes in brain chemistry brought about by social turbulence may help set a pattern in the brain for the expression of violence.

For example, Chicago psychiatrist Helen Morris has proposed that early beatings or lack of family supports may prevent the brain's hypothalamus—a powerful regulator of the body's hormonal and emotional systems—from developing adequately. This defect can occur because of faulty learning, which prevents the permanent assimilation of early patterning of emotional control over impulses. Beatings or birthing problems can cause enough trauma to the head to damage the hypothalamus, and thereby disrupt the brain's ability to inhibit unruly emotions. Morris points to studies of primates and other animals showing that the hypothalamus is crucial to the regulation of fear and rage.

As we have already seen, other researchers have noted that an upturn in the body's sense of readiness to respond to a perceived threat may be associated with higher than average levels of the hormone noradrenaline or with low levels of the brain chemical serotonin. Such findings suggest that there may be a biochemical breaking point in certain individuals at which they cause mayhem.

Physical damage to the brain may also mark the difference between a pent-up person who is occasionally violent and someone who turns his anger loose on strangers, as Richard Speck did in the summer of 1966.

Speck had some of the traits found in many mass murderers. He was the product of an impoverished and broken home; did poorly at school; became withdrawn in his teens; drank heavily; abused drugs; tortured animals; was obsessed with knives; fought with his peers; and regularly assaulted women, including his wife, who eventually left him. The tattoo on his left arm said "Born to Raise Hell."

Speck also suffered numerous head injuries, including a very hard, accidental, self-inflicted smash with a hammer when he was a child. At age fifteen, he ran head-first into a storefront awning. For years, Speck suffered terrible headaches, was impulsively violent, and experienced blackouts after he had committed an assault. When he returned to consciousness, he could not always recall what he had done.

Marvin Ziporyn, the doctor who studied Speck and wrote a book about his life, concluded that he was brain-damaged, that this damage led to instability and was exacerbated by inadequate parenting.

The combination of factors that led Speck to shoot eight nursing students remains elusive, although we do know that an apparent robbery attempt at their apartment went out of control. When one of the women spit in his face, he apparently became totally unglued and couldn't stop firing. It has also been suggested that the fact that one of the nurses resembled his ex-wife probably helped put him over the top.

Mass murderer Charles Whitman might also have suffered brain damage. After he killed his wife and mother, he climbed a high tower at the University of Texas at Austin, in August 1966, and began shooting. He killed thirteen people and wounded thirty-one others before a police marksman shot him. The autopsy showed that he had a tumor the size of a pecan in a region immediately above the brain stem.

Like many other mass murderers, Whitman had had a troubled childhood. He lived in fear of his father, who beat him and his mother. After a stint in the Marines that was marred by episodes of impulsive violence, Whitman began to notice changes in his personality. "I definitely feel as though there is something unusual in my mental state," he noted in a diary. Yet although he was considered to be at times difficult, he was well-liked by neighbors and friends.

But Whitman, by this time, felt life had little meaning. In a note he wrote before the killings, he again expressed his concerns about his mental state: "I don't really understand myself these days. I am supposed to be an average reasonable and intelligent young man. However, lately (I can't recall when it started) I have been a victim of many unusual and irrational thoughts. These thoughts constantly recur, and it requires a tremendous mental effort to concentrate on useful and progressive tasks." By this time, Whitman had already decided on his plan to kill.

Did the tumor in Whitman's brain contribute to his condition? Possibly. The panel of thirty-two experts convened by the state to study Whitman's medical file did only what panels of experts can do in the absence of hard evidence: they suggested that the tumor could have contributed, in some unknown way, to Whitman's murder spree. It was, at least, a plausible hypothesis, and one which challenges the notion that mass murderers are "monsters" or "evil."

For every mass murderer who kills and harms dozens or serial killer who feasts on his prey, there are countless others with deep and dangerous wounds that fester slowly. Our world of strife confirms the prejudices of those who live on the edge. Hatred is expressed on mainstream talk shows, in comedy clubs, in pamphlets, on the Internet: ethnic hatred, racial hatred, religious hatred, gender hatred, political hatred.

Even so, many people gather on anniversaries of mass murders to vow that they will not let such violence happen again. But mass murder will occur again and again. So will serial killing. These terrors are endemic to our way of life—in the inadequate way many people bring up their children and the way that many adults lose social supports as they try unsuccessfully to cope with social change.

All the while, society's immune system is being worn down by conflict. Inhibitions are being erased. Biological propensities for extreme violence are waiting to be unleashed. And there is even more potential for violence if there is physical damage to key emotional and judgment centers in the brain.

Meanwhile, our legal system, which adjudicates this violence, looks suspiciously on biologically oriented defenses, while holding firm to the unprovable premise that, with rare exceptions, each individual is accountable for his or her actions.

II

At the heart of our legal system is the doctrine of "personal responsibility." The idea has its roots in ancient supernatural beliefs, and is a staple of modern religion, packaged as a "soul" or "mind" separate from the physical body. It is an essence somewhere in the brain, yet apart from it, the ultimate organizer of experience and motive.

There is not a shred of scientific evidence that a human being has some innate or learned capacity to exert the kind of choice the term "responsibility" suggests. Such a notion ignores the power of culture to write itself on the human brain. It also fails to consider the human brain's power, built over many centuries of evolution, to steer behavior, including the emotions.

Yet the idea of "personal responsibility" is deeply entrenched in our political/legal/religious environment, perhaps because study of the interplay between the brain and culture is still very new: a viable workaday substitute for "personal responsibility" is embryonic, at best.

Nevertheless, there is growing turmoil in the courts because "personal responsibility" as a guiding concept is becoming less and less convincing in light of developments in brain science.

In the mid-1990s, it is still presumed that a person has the ability to determine "right" from "wrong." For instance, it is wrong to kill when the killing is not sanctioned by society. With the exception of provable accidents, such as inadvertent car crashes, or provable self-defense, to kill wrongfully often presupposes an intention to do so. One way to beat a first-degree murder charge is to declare in defense that the ability to determine right from wrong was intellectually impaired.

The concept of intellectual impairment assumes there is a definable "normalcy." There isn't.

At the extreme end of the normalcy continuum, legally speaking, is the concept of insanity, by reason of which an individual is *not* responsible for his or her actions: something in that individual prevented an understanding of the consequences of taking the action in question. The concept of legal insanity was codified more than a century ago, and a very narrow concept it is. Take, for example, the British case of serial killer Dennis Nilsen. He was arrested in 1983 after he had killed fifteen young men. As Nilsen described in his prison notebooks, he strangled the men, bathed them, dressed them and talked to them. His victims were his companions; he was lonely. When the bodies piled up, he crammed them beneath the floor, burned them or cut them up. He boiled the heads and flushed the flesh down the toilet. His defense of insanity, on the grounds that he suffered from an "abnormality of mind" whenever he killed, was rejected by the jury. Legally speaking, he knew what he was doing: The man who slept beside dismembered and decomposing bodies was perfectly sane. Nilsen was given a life sentence, with a recommendation that he remain jailed for at least twenty-five years.

In his biography of Nilsen, titled *Killing for Company*, Brian Masters rightly points to the verdict as a "crazy conclusion." In the postscript to the book, psychiatrist Anthony Storr, who has long studied human violence, concludes: "One thing which clearly emerges from the Nilsen trial is that both psychiatric classification of mental disorder and legal concepts relating to it are totally inadequate."

Over the years, the legal definition of insanity has been the subject of much debate. Opinion has ranged: some simply call the term "confusing"; some argue that, in the absence of definable brain damage, it is totally meaningless; others demand that it be dropped; and equally trenchant demands are made to extend its scope.

Today, some U.S. states keep the legal definition of insanity very strict, as do Canada and Britain, thereby ensuring that relatively few defense decisions base a case on insanity. Unless the defense can prove some bizarre chronic or acute incapacitation of reasoning ability, they might as well consider their killer client guilty as charged. (In Canada, when an individual charged with murder is considered way off the charts by both the prosecution and the defense, the case is usually settled without trial and the "insane" person is sent off to a psychiatric hospital.)

Some states, such as California, have broadened the insanity defense to allow for a claim of "diminished capacity," an example of how the law gradually shifts when it becomes increasingly apparent that a prevailing legal definition is wanting. From "diminished capacity" was born the "neurological defense," in which evidence from brain science is used to demonstrate that an individual who has suffered damage to the brain's limbic region can behave impulsively, even to the point of harming or killing another individual. This condition is referred to as "episodic dyscontrol."

In the 1960s, psychiatrist Frank Ervin and neurosurgeon Vernon Mark studied scores of individuals who experienced periodic rage attacks. They found that many of these men had dysfunctions deep in their temporal lobes. More recently, psychiatrist Anneliese Pontius has proposed on the basis of her clinical cases that some shy, loner types who are otherwise apparently healthy individuals may be susceptible to a brain seizure that can trigger killer behavior. Pontius theorizes that these men experience limbic overstimulation, which overwhelms the frontal lobes that normally hold our animalistic drives in check. She thinks that a powerful event triggers a memory of a bad experience in the susceptible person's life and kindles the seizure. She also considers the possibility that lesions in the limbic region can trigger both loner behavior and violence. The implication here, as in cases presented by Ervin and Mark, is that a wounded brain can trigger violent behavior.

The murder defense based on limbic malfunction has been intermittently successful; but what about dysfunctions that are not grounded in limbic disease? For instance, what about damage of the frontal lobes, the brain's powerful regulators of self-control. Here, the scientific data have depended largely on psychological tests showing such things as diminished learning and reasoning ability. Such research has had little effect: few non-limbic defenses lead to acquittal on the grounds of diminished responsibility.

That may change, however, as brain science investigates further the relationship between frontal-lobe dysfunction and violent behavior. The recent medical focus on the strange case of Phineas Gage is a modest step in that direction. Gage was a Vermont railroad worker in the 1800s whose personality changed markedly after an iron rod pierced his skull. Once a "balanced" individual, he began to exhibit behavior that was offensive and unpredictable. Gage's doctor documented the loss of balance "between his intellectual faculty and his animal propensities." Recent analysis of Gage's preserved skull confirms that he suffered damage to his frontal lobes.

Meanwhile, the boundaries of "diminished capacity" are being stretched by many new legal defenses. The optimistic view is to see these cases as representing a strong and inevitable challenge, however peculiar at times, to the unsubstantiated idea of "personal responsibility." The jaded view is that these courtroom shenanigans merely test what a lawyer can steal from a jury.

One such case involved the mental state of Colin Ferguson, who trapped about ninety people on the 5:33 P.M. Long Island Railroad train to Hicksville, New York, and used a semi-automatic to kill six strangers and injure nineteen others. Ferguson, a black man whose life had been on the skids, hated whites, Asians and "Uncle Tom Negroes." The mass murders were his revenge.

His lawyers planned a defense based on the combined effect of a mental disorder and "black rage," described as a mistrust and suspicion of outsiders by a victim of systemic racism. The announced strategy, particularly the "black rage" component, raised many eyebrows and inflamed those who believed it was, at best, hucksterism. Harvard lawyer and author Alan Dershowitz, for one, viewed it as another silly form of "abuse excuse."

Dershowitz believes that modern civilization functions because we believe strongly in personal responsibility. Without that belief, he argues, our legal structure would break down and our society would crumble into chaos and anarchy. This extreme position is certainly a conversation stopper, but it is not provable. It must be taken on faith—and most people are willing to do so. It is likely that, as more evidence on the shaping of personal violence emerges from the biological and behavioral sciences, our willingness to experiment with the legal system will gradually lead to significant change.

We certainly should not be satisfied with what happened to Ferguson. First, he fired his lawyers, and then defended himself in a mockery of a trial that showed him to be disoriented. He was, however, not legally insane and was therefore convicted of murder.

The belief that there are "monsters" among us who are driven by "evil" encourages our resolve to trap, punish and isolate them, to separate "them" from "us." Our hope ultimately to rid ourselves of the demons is an exercise in self-delusion. Violence is "us," extreme or otherwise.

The mass murderers and serial killers who make the news headlines are reminders to us to look within, to acknowledge our own potential for violence.

3

CONSEQUENCES OF THE "QUICK FIX" APPROACH TO VIOLENCE

7

Culture of Violence:

The Misinformed Campaign to Control or Eliminate Violent News and Entertainment Imagery

I

If it bleeds, it leads—the grinding principle of television news. Network news, local news, news magazines, tabloid shows and entertainment shows—all are preoccupied with "true crime," from famous trials to shoot-ups at the neighborhood grocery store.

In the movies, we learn to stab someone in the brain through an eye socket. On radio, former Watergate crook Gordon Liddy, Jr., explains how to win a shoot-out with federal agents. In home-video games, such as Mortal Kombat, the victor can rip out the loser's heart, barehanded. "Gangsta rap" recites explicit tales of sex, drugs and gangs, to a blazing beat. Do these images of violence contribute to our potential to express violent feelings and urges?

Can we realistically insist that our brains are not influenced by these images of violence?

These images are among the everyday stimuli processed by the brain into the electrical neuron charges and chemical sprays that shape behavior. It is one thing, however, to expect that a steady diet of violent imagery, presented, say, on television or in movies, will have an effect on our lives, and quite another to insist, as many do, that it is a major cause of societal violence.

Ongoing efforts to curb violence on television and in movies are misinformed about the range of cultural ingredients that help to facilitate violence. Television, for example, both reflects and reinforces societal norms and expectations. Sitcoms, talk shows, "family" shows, newscasts, and especially advertisements, emphasize a link between success and power. These messages fuel the desire to compete for financial rewards and status. They help maintain a societal structure of winners and losers, and thereby open the door to our potential for conflict and violence.

Seen in this much broader context, the proposed link between violent imagery and violent behavior is being vastly oversold. It is a political offering to convince a fearful public that there is a simple, available solution to violence. It also impedes understanding of how various forces can converge to produce violence.

Political interest in violent imagery presented on TV or in movies often intensifies after a well-publicized brutal murder. It is a strategy to suggest to the public that something may be done to prevent yet another tragedy. For example, the 1993 murder of two-year-old James Bulger by ten-year-olds Jon Venables and Robert Thompson focused British attention on ultra-violent home-videos, which one of the killers may have watched. The judge even referred to this possibility in sentencing the two boys.

Several British politicians took the opportunity to suggest that scenes of extreme violence should be banned from videos and TV screens to protect the young. (Just for good measure, the politicians also suggested a ban on explicit sex.) Their proposal involved having the British Board of Film Classification cut material from home viewing that was "likely to cause grave offence to a reasonable person."

James Ferman, the board's director, refused to cooperate and chided the politicians for not considering that films were already heavily censored in Britain. He challenged the British government to conduct an evaluation of media images of violence, if, in fact, the goal was to determine the nature of "subconscious influences on behavior." He then tweaked the politicians, asking whether they knew, for instance, that Ian Brady, one of the duo of English serial killers known to have committed the "Moors Murders," had read the sexually violent works of the Marquis de Sade.

Several months later, a report on violent videos issued by the child-development unit at Nottingham University, and signed by twenty-five psychologists and pediatricians, concluded that "nasties" were damaging to the young and recommended that they be made unavailable for home viewing. By then, however, the Bulger trial was fading from public awareness, and concern about censorship tempered the political resolve to restrict home-viewing access to scenes of torment and carnage.

Across the Atlantic, the portrayal of violence in various entertainment media, including videos, and the effects on human behavior were also getting simple-minded political attention. The focus was on television, and the medium's critics, including several in the U.S. Senate, were pushing for the reduction of images of violence in everything from cartoon shows to murder mysteries to movie reruns. Free-speech advocates, as usual, took issue with such proposals.

Under steady political pressure, however, TV network executives decided in December 1992 that they would more carefully monitor the violent content of their shows. By June 1993, the networks had announced that, in the coming fall season, they would issue a warning prior to shows they deemed violent. Only *NYPD Blue*, a police drama on ABC, qualified for the warning.

One month later, U.S. Attorney General Janet Reno warned the TV industry that the federal government would step in if the networks failed to discipline themselves, the same message television has heard since the first congressional hearing on TV violence in 1952. Recent congressional attention has coincided with a widespread and growing public fear about violence in real life.

In Canada, unlike in the United States and Britain, the government didn't meet with impressive resistance in its efforts to curb some television violence. In the aftermath of Marc Lepine's murder of fourteen female engineering students at the École Polytechnique in Montreal late in 1989, the Canadian Radio-Television and Telecommunications Commission, the federal licensing agency, began to study the relationship between television and violence. In 1992, the agency, believing that there was strong scientific evidence of a link, convinced the indigenous broadcast industry, via the Canadian Association of Broadcasters, to amend its television-violence code.

The result will likely be fewer depictions of gratuitous violence (i.e., instances not essential to plot and character) based on race, gender, religion, sexual orientation, color, ethnic origin, age or mental or physical disability. Similar restrictions apply to children's shows involving real-life characters. In animated shows, violence cannot be a central theme, nor can a dangerous act, such as the use of matches, be depicted, lest it be imitated by children.

One reason for Canadian acceptance of these restrictions may be that most Canadian couch potatoes can easily pick up channels from the United States and elsewhere, so they do not feel put-upon by occasional censorship. Canadians also are thought to be generally more willing than Americans to give up some personal freedoms for peace and social order.

Except for a handful of TV producers, academics and media columnists, Canadians didn't raise much public fuss when the federal government announced in 1995 that TV sets would soon come equipped with a computer chip (known as the "V-chip") that could be programmed to block out violent programs, particularly those that might be seen by children. There will be a ratings system developed by broadcasters that will determine the level of violent content in each program, enabling viewers to set their chip according to their individual level of comfort.

Similar plans are under way in the United States, where TV sets are scheduled to be equipped with the chip starting in 1998. In February 1996, Congress passed the Communications Decency Act, which sets up a television-ratings system. It will require a committee to rate more than 600,000 hours of television each year. In Britain, politicians have expressed interest in following North America's example, as have some of their colleagues in the European Parliament and, more recently, Australia. Some of this V-chip mania is political posturing in response to episodes of violence by lone gunmen. In Britain, the V-chip gained political appeal following the killing of fourteen children in Dunblane. In Australia, the government expressed more interest in television-censorship controls soon after the massacre of thirty-five people in southern Tasmania.

The opposition to this certain change in TV viewing, particularly in the United States, is twofold. Some critics point out that the ratings system will not only become difficult to create, given the subjective nature of defining violence, but will also become a political football, used for politicians' and vocal minorities' lobbying efforts. Second, test runs in Canada have indicated that it will likely be difficult to deliver a problem-free and consumer-friendly V-chip.

But there is a more fundamental problem with the V-chip: its promised utility is based on an extremely narrow view of why people behave violently.

I expect the wrong-headed political preoccupation with violence on television and in movies to continue, as there will always be someone who watched a television show and committed a brutal act shortly thereafter.

For instance:

- A two-year-old girl died when her five-year-old brother played with matches and set the house on fire. The boy is said to have imitated a scene on the TV show *Beavis and Butt-head*.
- Two girls, ages eleven and twelve, forced two younger children to have sex. They say their curiosity was aroused by videos.
- A rash of shootings followed a California premiere of the movie *Boyz N the Hood*.

Critics of media violence typically seize on such cases of violence that appear to be the result of a specific stimulus. Television is then blamed for everything from teens carrying knives to drive-by shootings. If TV isn't demonized as the direct cause of violent behavior, it is usually declared to be a principal contributor.

One argument in support of this thesis is that images of violence gradually overpower our natural resistance to violence. This view is found in Lieutenant-Colonel Dave Grossman's book, *On Killing*. In it, he maintains that images of violent behavior wear us down and, in effect, train us to view the inflicting of pain and suffering as entertainment. "We are learning to kill and we are learning to like it," he claims. Grossman compares the desensitization caused by violent imagery on the screen with the conditioning of troops to kill in battle. In both cases, he argues, the resistance to violence can be broken down. However, in the military, violence is choreographed by authority; in society, there is unrestrained desensitization. The avenging hero depicted in the movies by the likes of Sylvester Stallone and Arnold Schwarzenegger often operates outside the law. Grossman sees such tacit approval of uncontrolled violence as a major threat to our civilization.

Grossman draws some support from bestselling novelist John Grisham, who has waged a campaign against "glamorized casual mayhem and bloodlust" in movies. He has championed a lawsuit brought by Patsy Ann Byers, a Louisiana woman brutalized by a burglar said to have been inspired to act after viewing the movie *Natural Born Killers*. The suit claims that the moviemakers, including director Oliver Stone, should have realized that the orgy of violence in the movie would cause some individuals to copy some of the acts in real life. Grisham contends that a violent movie should be seen as a product with the power to harm.

While Oliver Stone acknowledges that his movie could have heightened someone's susceptibility to enact violence, he defends his film by pointing to numerous factors that can shape a propensity for violence over time, particularly a psychiatric history, and drug abuse, as was possibly the case of the burglar who harmed Patsy Ann Byers.

Grisham's view that a violent movie can lead to harm may indeed be accurate in some instances. Yes, some individuals might be pushed over the edge by a fury of violent imagery. But we cannot predict which individuals, which images, and under what circumstances.

Grossman's likening of entertainment violence to conditioning and desensitizing techniques in the military suggests he does not understand societal dynamics. Military training is highly focused; it is therefore not comparable to behavior shaped in a culture of diverse inputs, including that of family, friends, schools, neighborhoods and everyday stresses and strains. Grossman makes a strong case for why each and every individual is potentially capable of killing and maiming, a point of view that I strongly share; but his analysis of the role of entertainment violence in the making of a killer is annoyingly simplistic.

Our news and entertainment world, as should be evident to these and other critics of violent imagery, is an open tap of messages. One constantly running message is a fundamental value of daily life: accumulate wealth and the world will be your oyster. This message floods commercials, sitcoms, the soaps and *The Monday Night Movie*. Images of violence are merely a tiny boat on a sea of consumerism. The message is also a direct consequence of the powerful market forces that drive our economy. Such a message, also known these days as a "meme," a basic unit of information competing with other units, has become embedded in our culture.

Our consumer society teaches the young that individuals are measured by their wealth, and that failure to achieve prosperity means you are a loser. This message plays a major part in our development of a sense of self. In the consumer culture, the brain's complex electrochemical structures receive a steady input of "Through buying goods you will define yourself." Children begin to pine for the "good life." They become consumers-in-waiting, urged on by messages on billboards, trucks and signs in sports arenas; on buses and taxi cabs; and on shopping bags.

Not having the "good life" is bound to cause anxiety. Blocked efforts to channel energies into the marketplace may engender hostility. If you cannot afford the expensive sports shoes that multimillionaire basketball star Michael Jordan endorses, why not steal them? Or why not make some quick money selling drugs? And if you cause someone harm in achieving your goal, well, tough. The cult of commodity obeys no higher authority: losers in the economic wars try to become winners.

In this much broader context than critics of television violence allow, entertainment acts to counter feelings of powerlessness. Television holds out visions of the Good Life, even if the one route to it is through deception and, if necessary, force. Rap music gives vent to frustrations, and movie bloodbaths demonstrate that anything is possible if you have enough firepower.

Critics of television do not appreciate the medium's overall power because they do not acknowledge the history of their own consumer culture. Early Americans heard plenty about how hard work could lead from obscurity to affluence. They were ripe for manipulation when the modern corporation early this century set out to produce customers who would never be satisfied: they would always "need" one more item to be happy.

Radio, mass-circulation magazines (about fifty by 1947) and newspapers conveyed the corporate messages to millions. And then came television. By the 1960s, advertisers were relying heavily on research that claimed to decipher the hidden yearnings of consumers. In *The New Industrial State*, economist John Kenneth Galbraith explained that the business of the modern corporation was managing consumer demand. In this he echoed sociologist C.W. Mills's contention that carefully designed media formulas were telling people who they were, what they should be and how they could succeed. The result of this manipulation, according to political theorist Herbert Marcuse, was the media creation of a "happy consciousness," the illusion that consumerism was the path to contentment. Children were certainly not immune to the messages of the corporate image-makers. Some social critics, including David Reisman, author of *The Lonely Crowd*, warned that children were being manipulated into becoming "consumer moppets."

Today, corporations spend more than $20 billion annually on television advertising; and, indeed, television's primary purpose is to provide captive audiences for corporate messages. But the many millions of individuals whose lives are not turning out to be as advertised need different strategies to achieve power and happiness. For some, this fantasy world of power can be obtained only by force. The fantasy world of sex can be obtained only by rape. This Great Divide, not the violence shown on the tube, should be our primary concern.

Some people believe that a major technology shift is turning the culture onto a better course. The digital revolution, they say, will soon make television, as we know it, dead as a doornail. "Cyberspace," the worldwide, computer-generated communications playland, is giving television the boot. George Gilder, who writes on "television and beyond," accurately calls television a "tool of tyrants." By that, he means that it is a technology that enables "masters" to "rule over huge masses of people." Gilder, a political conservative, may find it inappropriate to question some of the aims and consequences of free enterprise, but it is clear that the masters are the advertisers.

There is little discussion by the wizards of the new cyberspace, including Gilder and Nicholas Negroponte, author of the bestselling *Being Digital*, about the next era of economic hardship, social divisions, violent imagery and real-world violence. They do concede, however, that there will be digital winners and non-digital losers.

Negroponte is very enthusiastic about the Internet, that worldwide telephone web of intercommunicating computers. What began as a Pentagon defense against a nuclear attack is now a vast union of subscribers. By the year 2000, it is estimated, 1 billion people will be "on line."

The "Net" reflects what our culture has to offer, including available goods and services. It is, in large part, a huge free-market shopping and entertainment mall.

Advertisers on the Internet often target "cybertots" as aggressively as they do boomers. The Center for Media Education, a non-profit group in Washington, D.C., informs us, after a six-month review of websites, that the marketing techniques in this new land of wonder are "manipulative, deceptive and exploitive." In one example the center provides, children enter contests and provide details about their families and lifestyles. Then they get blitzed by product-oriented E-mail from some of the "characters" in the contests.

No, the Net is not likely to save us from the drone of "good life" propaganda. Indeed, the electronic highway already has more "billboards" than all the world's blacktops combined. Each time we take the journey, we can look forward to the most dizzying array of corporate messages ever assembled.

II

The narrow focus on violent news and entertainment images, often without regard to the complex web of influences people face in daily life, is reflected in the large body of science, without breadth or context, mired in popular psychology and statistical machination. This is science suited to political expediency, not intelligent social policy. And it is to this body of limited evidence that critics of television violence usually turn for support of their arguments. This body of science reveals some of the processes that might occur as individuals live in a matrix of messages, including violent ones. But it should not be interpreted as simplistically as it was in a full-page ad that appeared on November 30, 1993, in *USA Today*. Sponsored by the American Family Association, a group claiming almost 2 million families as members, the ad read: "WE ARE OUTRAGED. How dare you say TV violence and sex have no consequences!" The ad then asked rhetorically whether the "moral rot on Oprah, Geraldo and Donahue" had any effect on "millions of kids," and referred to "thousands of studies and 27 congressional hearings on TV violence over 20 years."

The ad, however, was less than judicious. "Thousands of studies" do *not* prove that television fosters violence in *daily life*. The data do not even prove that television violence is a principal contributor to real-life violence.

Consider the studies aimed at determining the so-called effects of television imagery on behavior. For example, children watched a very aggressive cartoon character; then they were tested for signs of aggression. Their level of aggression was then compared with that of children who watched a gentle cartoon character. The study would usually conclude that the aggressive images produced more signs of aggressive behavior.

These studies do demonstrate that, under controlled laboratory conditions, individuals react measurably to images of violence. There is no doubt about that: these images can potentially have some impact on the brain, especially over time, if repeated enough, especially from an early age. But to extrapolate from the controlled world of the laboratory to the complex dynamics of how inputs from daily life affect the brain is quite a stretch.

To further the argument that repeated images of violence can become neurally patterned, or "hard-wired," in the brain, the critics of television violence refer to the numerous hours children spend watching television. They suggest that television viewing is a very passive activity leading children to develop a trancelike state and to become highly suggestible to violent imagery.

Let's look at this more closely: American and Canadian children, on average, are said to watch three to four hours of television daily. (Some apparently watch for as much as seventy-five hours per week.) They view acts of violence on the news, in cop series and in movies.

The American Psychological Association says that the typical child will view 100,000 acts of violence before completing elementary school. It would take championship-level channel-surfing to reach that level, and, indeed, other estimates are far lower—about 30,000. Without question, however, this is a strong dose of violent imagery.

But is it only violence they watch? Clearly not. They will also get input from tens of thousands of commercials promoting the consumer "good life" and from "family" shows that sell the values of fierce competitiveness and markers of social and financial success. Why don't we hear about their potential impact on a developing brain and their contribution to violent behavior?

Studies within the laboratory or the home fail for the same reason: they do not control for, or take into account, the wide array of stimulation that individuals receive from different sources. Some studies show a positive correlation between strong exposure to television in childhood (particularly in preadolescence) and later physical aggressiveness. But what types of television messages contribute to this correlation is unclear.

As an example of how problematic these studies can be, let's examine research involving a small town in Canada named "Notel," which did not receive television until 1973. Notel was, in research parlance, a "virgin community" for a study of how television affects behavior.

The research design of the study pitted Notel against two supposedly similar communities that already had television. First-and second-grade students in all three communities were observed over a two-year period for signs of aggressive behavior—hitting, shoving and biting. In the two years after television was introduced into their community, the aggressive behavior of the children of Notel rose 160 percent. The aggression rates did not change significantly in the control communities.

But the study's focus—on the *content* of television—was too narrow. In sociology methodology, whenever you try to determine the effects of an independent variable (in this case, television) on a dependent variable (violence) in a complex social system (Notel), there are numerous, and uncontrolled, factors that can skew the results. Indeed, one would expect the introduction of a new and powerful technology into a community to have an array of unpredictable and unmeasurable effects on daily living. For example, the researchers could have considered the impact of television on such things as community patterns, household patterns, parenting patterns, sibling relationships, friendship patterns, eating and sleeping habits, and schooling practices. Yet the study explored none of these aspects. As for the lack of significant change in the control communities, they may have reached a relatively stabilized accommodation of the direct and indirect effects of television. This too was never investigated.

Another example of science often cited as proof of television's impact on violent behavior is packaged with some surprising speculation in a paper published in *The Journal of the American Medical Association* on June 10, 1992, by Dr. Brandon Centerwall. Formerly in the Department of Psychiatry and Behavioral Science at the University of Washington, in Seattle, and now in private practice, Centerwall compared homicide rates among whites in the United States and South Africa with total homicide rates in Canada. The goal was to show the effects of television. In the United States, the rate increased by 93 percent, from 3.0 per 100,000 population in 1945 to 5.8 in 1974. He found a similar rate increase in Canada for roughly the same time period. In South Africa, where television was banned prior to 1975, the homicide rate decreased by 7 percent. (Centerwall offers no explanation for this decline.) After the introduction of television, the South African rate rose sharply. In 1987, it reached 6.8 homicides per 100,000 population, an increase of 130 percent over the 2.5 figure in 1974.

Centerwall reasons that a time lag between the introduction of television (in 1951 in the United States and Canada) and a homicide-rate increase indicates that children exposed to the medium show the effects as adults. The proof, he suggests, is the difference in South African rates before and after the introduction of television.

To his credit, Centerwall asks whether he isolated the effects of television from other (independent) variables. As an example of proof that he has done so, he points to the book-publishing, newspaper, radio and movie industries in South Africa as not having had a discernible effect on the homicide rate, prior to the introduction of television. And, in another analysis, he feels confident that he ruled out factors such as changes in age distribution, urban development, economic conditions, alcohol consumption, capital punishment, civil unrest and gun availability as viable explanations for the changes in homicide rates.

But he did not separate the impact of television from such everyday-life variables as the emerging patterns of crime and poverty, stress, drug abuse and feelings of powerlessness, and the cultural norms and behavioral patterns these variables can help generate. Most likely he could not have done so, given the complexity of the data that would be required.

(It's worth noting that, in 1995, after Nelson Mandela won election in South Africa, the murder rate soared to 18,983 per annum, an average of 52 people per day. Compare this rate of 87.5 per 100,000 to the rate of 5.8 after television was introduced in that country. Is television responsible for this recent rise? Or might the vast economic gulf between white and black, settling of political and ethnic accounts, and prevailing social conditions play an important role in the escalation of homicide?)

In short, Centerwall's research boils down to a guess that television is the culprit behind the increase in homicide rates.

It is his final conclusions in the *JAMA* paper, however, that are truly eye-catching. He declares on the basis of the U.S. data that the introduction of television in that country "caused a subsequent doubling of the homicide rate." And he explains that "long-term childhood exposure to television is a causal factor behind approximately one-half of the homicides committed in the United States or approximately 10,000 homicides annually."

Then Centerwall takes this leap: "Although the data are not as well developed for other forms of violence, they indicate that exposure to television is also a causal factor behind a major proportion—perhaps one half—of rapes, assaults, and other forms of interpersonal violence in the United States."

Then he fantasizes in the guise of science: "If, hypothetically, television technology had never been developed, there would today be 10,000 fewer homicides each year in the United States, 70,000 fewer rapes, and 700,000 fewer injurious assaults." Again, Centerwall assumes, without supporting data, that the impact of television on social behavior can be separated from other influences.

But bad science doesn't stop people from using Centerwall's data to support their apparent political agenda. On May 31, 1994, in the *Wall Street Journal*, Irving Kristol, a conservative commentator, cited Centerwall's epidemiology and endorsed the restriction of some freedoms so that television broadcasting can be limited. "Modest limits on adult liberties," he wrote, "ought to be perfectly acceptable if they prevent tens of thousands of our children from growing up into criminal adults . . ." Then he makes this telling and scary comment: "We don't really need social science to confirm what common sense and common observations tell us to be the case."

Kristol's observations are certainly common—and wrong. He refers to bad science and ends with no science.

The search for simple solutions to violence is mere political expediency trolling for scientific validation of the notion that television violence and entertainment violence in general are major causes of societal violence. This fantasy quest unfortunately will likely continue for years to come. Its net effect will be haphazard censorship, rather than a reduction or a better understanding of violence.

In the chapters ahead, we shall observe further how other simple-minded solutions to violence are being politically favored and how they are being sold shamelessly to a fearful public. These strategies represent nothing less than a move farther along the path toward totalitarian rule.

8

The Gun Society:

The Gun as a Service Tool for Human Violence

I

Nations differ significantly in the way they view and control the use of guns. Japan is close to being gun-free. The United States is at the opposite end of the spectrum; perhaps as many as 40 to 50 percent of American households own at least one gun. Canada holds the middle ground.

Japan has one of the world's lowest violent-crime rates; the United States has one of the highest. Is there, then, a causal relationship between gun ownership and violent crime?

One would think so, judging by some of the claims made by gun-control advocates in the United States and elsewhere. Yet why is it that, Switzerland, for example, where about 27 percent of all households own a gun, has such a low violent-crime rate? Can historical and social factors help explain why some become high- and others low-violent-crime societies?

Neither Switzerland nor Japan has a vast, frustrated underclass, as does the United States, the *New York Times* suggests. However, both have small segments of their populations that might be characterized as "outcast," and they are responsible for much of the crime.

Moreover, nations such as Sri Lanka, Jamaica, Mexico and Russia make it very difficult to obtain a gun legally, but all have high overall rates of homicide.

Nations that have raging gun-control debates focusing on crime statistics, including the United States and Canada, rarely engage in societal self-evaluation. Yes, guns appear to promote violence; but it is hardly the full story.

In the gun society, most individuals do not perceive guns as emblematic of a culture that clings to primitivism, both by evolutionary design and by historical chance. Focusing primarily on the gun as a major cause of violence significantly diminishes the opportunity to better understand violence.

Today, when the U.S. population is close to 300 million, there are some 216 million guns in private hands, including 67 million handguns and between 1 and 3 million semi-automatic assault-type weapons. Each year, about 15,000 homicides are committed with guns; as well, more than 600,000 gun-related felonies are reported, including assault, rape and robbery. There are 14 homicides for every 100,000 American men. (Compare this with 2.2 in Canada, and slightly more than 1.0 in Britain.) The U.S. rate of homicides by women is about 4.0; the overall rate of other industrialized nations ranges somewhere between 0.3 and about 2.0 per 100,000.

This U.S. preoccupation with guns and violence has a long history. Americans have always used the gun as a means of both self-protection and aggression. The nation's founding was a result of insurrection; its expansion was achieved by a genocidal land-grab from Native Americans. In frontier days, self-protection was primarily a private responsibility. Then the country was torn by a civil war. With growing urbanization, city-dwellers armed themselves, sometimes at the urging of politicians and police commissioners. Today, drug wars are common on the streets of the decaying inner cities.

Efforts to limit gun use also have a long history, but have produced very dubious results. On the frontier, where people wore guns, lawmen would sometimes insist that cowboys check their weapons when they arrived in town. It was, in effect, an early form of local violence control. There were other attempts to temper the use of guns, such as the handgun prohibition in Georgia in 1837, which the state Supreme Court struck down as an infringement of the right to bear arms.

More modern efforts reflect both the transformation from a rural to an urban society, and grass-roots political populism. Originating in 1891 as a movement to represent agrarian concerns, populism looked to the federal government to right economic and social wrongs. After the Civil War, crime, poverty and overcrowding became common in cities, and populism also gave rise to a reform impulse to rid the nation of sin, corruption and moral decay. This era produced, on one hand, the "muckrakers," such as Upton Sinclair and Lincoln Steffens, whose probing research produced searing exposés of corporate corruption and exploitation, and, on the other, numerous cultural-reformist groups, including the General Federation of Women's Clubs, whose major contribution to the debate was a ban on the tango and the Hesitation Waltz.

The common element in these groups was a faith that American society, with its odd mix of entrepreneurial, laissez-faire spirit and moral activism, could be humanized through education, strong legal action and codes of conduct. (This vision was not unlike that of the Puritans, who believed that, because law was rooted in the nature of things, it was inevitable that law would become a *moral* device to purge the nation of its social transgressions.) This spirit would become embedded in a criminal code that regulated behavior, including homosexuality, prostitution and the use of alcohol and recreational drugs. Moral exhortation in the form of law would also address gun ownership.

Around the turn of the century, the frequent shoot-'em-ups in the cities became a target for reformers. The turbulence in New York State, which included the 1901 assassination of President William McKinley and the 1910 wounding of New York City mayor William Gaynor, resulted in the precedent-setting Sullivan Act of 1911. It required having a police permit to buy and/or own a handgun or other concealable weapon in New York State. Other states adopted similar laws.

Since then, the numerous federal and state gun laws reflect both a continued faith in the reformist ideal that legislation checks bad behavior and a knee-jerk political reaction to public fears about murder and guns.

The extent of gun ownership and easy illegal access to guns in the United States should suggest that, given the numbers, gun control has made as little sense as banning alcohol. Prohibition does not have a good track record in the free-wheeling United States. (Alcohol prohibition began there as an assertion of the rural religious mind against the secular urban life. Soon the "drys" were determined to regulate human morality; but the legal coercion clearly didn't pay off, except for Al Capone and other bootleggers, who, in classic American entrepreneurial fashion, saw a market opportunity and filled it.)

The control of drugs, likewise a product of the reformist impulse early this century, has also been a dismal failure. Predictably, black-market gunrunners supply the weapons for the drug wars. In some neighborhoods, you can get a gun quicker than you can a pizza. All told, it is estimated that five of six guns used in crimes in the United States are obtained illegally.

There is no question that guns cause widespread damage. A 1995 report from the Centers for Disease Control and Prevention in Atlanta indicates that, every year, nearly 100,000 people in the United States are hospitalized for gunshot wounds. And, every year, about 18,000 people use a gun to commit suicide. Intentional and unintentional injuries related to gun use cost more than $14 billion annually. There is also evidence, according to the U.S. Justice Department, that hand-gun violence is increasing.

It is not surprising that carnage on such a scale motivates the fight for gun-control legislation. But the cumulative data on guns and violence offer no reassuring evidence that firearm control has curbed overall violence and crime in American society. Nor is there strong reason to expect that more restrictive legislation will turn the tide.

But evidence is never persuasive in politically or emotionally based arguments. In recent years, for example, lobbying after the killings of former U.S. president John Kennedy, his brother Robert, and Martin Luther King, Jr., resulted in a 1968 federal act to tighten controls on interstate gun shipment and the importation of non-sporting guns. Legislation also followed the attempted assassination of former U.S. president Ronald Reagan on March 31, 1981. That day, John Hinckley, Jr., using a $29 handgun known as a "Saturday night special," shot press secretary James Brady in the head, causing neurological damage. Over the years, the wheelchair-bound Brady, who has limited use of his limbs and voice, together with his wife, Sarah, fought for handgun control, and finally achieved victory with the so-called Brady Bill in December 1993. The bill requires a five-day waiting period and a background check for anyone wishing to buy a handgun. (Other federal laws prevent minors, convicted felons, drug addicts, the mentally ill and illegal aliens from owning guns.) When the bill was signed, Brady said: "Twelve years ago, my life was changed forever by a disturbed young man with a gun. Until that time, I had not thought about gun control or the need for gun control. Maybe if I had done so, I wouldn't be stuck with these damn wheels." Perhaps.

Yet most Americans, James and Sarah Brady included, seem ill disposed to deal with the social contingencies that can promote violence. Gun reformism as a way to control violence is not being coupled with social and economic reformism, but with law-and-orderism. Gun-control advocates seem to believe that violence is a technical problem and that gun control can be an effective solution. They, like the reformers at the turn of the century, appear to have faith in the nation's ability to rid itself of its deep troubles without changing an economic system that relegates huge numbers of its people to a life of poverty, conflict and violence. They embody the spirit of former president Herbert Hoover, who vowed to conquer poverty *with the help of God* rather than a shift in the distribution of wealth.

The National Rifle Association is America's pro-gun champion. The 124-year-old organization, whose membership numbers 3.5 million, essentially divides the American population into the law-abiding and the criminal. It vigorously promotes the freedom of law-abiding citizens to use guns to defend themselves against criminals. The NRA also contends that better policing and longer prison terms can reduce violent activities of criminals. Alternatively, just *keep them away from us and throw away the key*. This simplistic world-view precludes discussion of how poverty and lack of employment opportunity can lead to adaptive maneuvers that sustain crime and violence. The NRA is not in the business of understanding violence, only in promoting defense systems against it.

The NRA once concerned itself mainly with sporting guns; now it vigorously promotes self-defense. The group's rhetoric has also become more extreme. In a fundraising letter sent out in the spring of 1995, it described federal advocates of limiting gun use as "jackbooted government thugs."

The NRA appears quite moderate when compared with the gun-worshipping neo-Nazis, survivalists, militias and other rightist groups in their bunkers throughout the United States. These people, usually members of the disaffected middle and working classes, are the philosophical and religious descendants of the Americans who opposed Franklin D. Roosevelt's New Deal as a tool of communism, and who believed the poor deserved to be poor because they were incompetent. Some of these "patriots" couple their gun advocacy with diatribes against racial, religious and ethnic minorities.

On the gun-show circuit, they sell their polemics and federal-government-bashing newsletters and bumper stickers. On their computer networks and radio talk shows, they offer advice on how to fend off an invasion of federal watchdogs and prevent the inevitable takeover of America by the armies of the United Nations.

Fearful that the "enemy" will steal their freedom and life opportunities, they don combat fatigues and engage in military training, believing that the gun is an effective defense. Some would rather die fighting than give up their handgun or semi-automatic.

In light of these trends, it isn't surprising that more Americans than ever want to pack guns. Media reports of violence dominate news coverage and have generally not made it clear that *extreme* violence, such as assault and murder, *on the streets* is largely concentrated in areas of high poverty and population density.

No matter. Some thirty-one states allow citizens without a prior history of police or psychiatric run-ins to carry concealed weapons. Other states have a requirement to show need. But, in Vermont, *anyone* can carry a gun without a license. So far, about 5 percent of the population *legally* carry a gun. It is probable that a much higher percentage will by the turn of the century, as more states will make it easier to do so and gun manufacturers (with help from the NRA) campaign to arm the nation. (The industry is designing small guns to appeal to women. As a group, women remain a largely untapped market, both as gun users and as potential NRA members. Full-page NRA ads have encouraged women to "refuse to be a victim" and to sign up for "empowerment.")

Both sides of the debate on whether guns can be successfully used for self-defense typically present statistical assessments and methodological opinions, which offer no clear victory. The available data are sparse and unconvincing. Gun advocates argue that an armed society will deter robbers, rapists and murderers. Their opponents counter that concealed guns breed violence: that people use them less inhibitedly, and that accidental deaths and suicides occur more frequently.

The titan of the pro-gun side has been Gary Kleck, a criminologist at Florida State University. He estimates that, several millions of times each year, people use guns to defend themselves successfully against threat or criminal intent. According to his data, just showing a gun often wards off danger. He concludes that gun ownership deters crime and increases the likelihood that victims will survive unscathed. Kleck gathered his data principally through telephone surveys, then extrapolated his results to the total population.

Such surveys are, of course, the bane of sociology, as there is no way to determine how honest or specific the respondents are. Indeed, other surveys, which may be no more or less reliable, suggest that far fewer crime victims use guns to protect themselves. One national crime survey puts the figure at about 80,000 per year. Kleck, however, insists that his research methods are dependable; in any event, he argues that more gun-control measures deprive people of the means to protect self and home, while potential intruders have access to the illegal weapons of their choice.

Arthur Kellerman, Director of the Emory University School of Public Health, reaches a very different conclusion on the basis of his research. He finds that gun ownership is a menace: guns in the home are used forty-three times more often to kill someone in the family or a friend than to deal with an invader. (His critics, including Kleck, argue that a true measure of comparative risk requires an investigation of how often guns provide benefit, not how often they are associated with death.)

From one study, Kellerman deduced that homeowners rarely use their guns for self-protection; but he admits that his data cannot tell him if the homeowners in the study actually had guns and/or had the opportunity to reach for their guns. As historically guns have been most concentrated in rural areas and in high-conflict neighborhoods, Kellerman, like Kleck, has no real idea what his figures tell him. At best, they can be used to take an educated guess. Those who are pro-gun tend to quote Kleck; the no-gun lobby looks to Kellerman's data. Take your pick.

When all is said and done, the debate over whether a gun in the home, holster, attaché case or purse provides personal safety or creates danger may be academic. Chances are that new gun users find it comforting to *feel* that they can protect themselves against harm, or that guns are synonymous with bravery and what it is to be American.

The rhetoric of bravery is a throwback to America's early days. The British and Native American enemies have long been vanquished: only the criminals remain. Trouble is, we are told by Real Americans, most citizens haven't the guts to draw their guns; therefore, violent crime continues to engulf the nation. Simple as that.

In an emotional appeal to the Real American hidden in every wimp, Jeffrey Snyder, a Washington-based lawyer, flies the flag of human individuality and self-worth. Who can argue with those qualities? Who wants indignity or enslavement when threatened? Snyder's analysis in the fall 1993 issue of the *The Public Interest*, a journal of social and political commentary, however, shows the limits of his understanding of violence. "Crime is rampant," he writes, "because the law-abiding, each of us, condone it, excuse it, permit it, submit to it. We permit and encourage it . . . The defect is there, in our character. We are a nation of cowards and shirkers."

Snyder is naive. It is not because Americans are cowards and shirkers that crime and violence are rampant; rather, it is because crime and violence are built into the structure and driving force of America. Yet such romantic yearnings of Snyder and his co-achievers on the right, as well as shallow thinking on both sides of the debate, block needed reforms to loosen the oppressiveness in the socio-economic structure and free constructive energies in the populace.

Snyder, however, may be right, as Kleck might, in proposing that there are more benefits than disadvantages in carrying a gun and in using it, if necessary—at least, on the *personal* level. But arming the populace won't rid America of its daily horrors, as Snyder would like us to believe.

II

Americans are not alone in perpetuating widespread misunderstanding of the relationship between guns and violence. When it comes to the art of self-delusion, Canadians run a very close second. However, because Canadians do not have a historical preoccupation with self-protection, there is much less patriotic rhetoric to wade through.

Having a population roughly 10 percent that of the United States, it is a rule of thumb that Canadians have 10 percent of anything found south of the border. (It is not unreasonable, for example, to estimate the prevalence of some diseases in this manner.) When it comes to guns, however, the statistics do not pan out. In Canada, there are about 3 million gun owners in a population of about 27 million. They own an estimated 7 million guns. This is about half the per-capita figure in the United States. Moreover, in Canada, relatively few individuals claim that their rifles, shotguns and handguns are for self-protection. Canadian gun owners are mostly hunters, target-shooters or collectors. Canadians do not believe that they have a natural right to bear arms, nor is any such right codified in law. And there is little history of Canadians needing to defend their homes against invaders. (When there has been, the invaders were Americans.)

Canada's homicide rate of 2.2 per 100,000 population is roughly one-fifth that of the United States. (About 1,400 Canadians die each year of gunshot wounds, compared with about 26,000 Americans); and the Canadian rate has declined by about 27 percent since the late 1970s.

In 1995, however, the House of Commons, after much bitter public debate, passed a bill in aid of better gun control. Its purpose was to enable the police to track weapons by having all guns registered, much like automobiles. The idea was to keep them out of the hands of criminals and the mentally unstable. The bill's advocates also pledged it would help deter crime and violence, particularly in the cities.

This government maneuver against crime and violence mimics the U.S. action. In December 1989, Canadians were outraged by the murder of fourteen women at the École Polytechnique in Montreal. The event unleashed public fury against the availability of guns, particularly military-type weapons. The gunman, Marc Lepine, had used a Ruger Mini-14, a semi-automatic. The reaction to his heinous crime was understandable, but the results were more emotional than practical. Mass slaughters are rare in Canada; and, as individuals can gain access to illegal weapons or those housed by the military, restrictions on guns cannot prevent such violence.

Much of the commentary on the slaughter in Montreal confused the lack of restrictions on weapons with a lack of control of *violence*. This confusion is also typical of the debate in the United States. In both countries, the focus appears to be on a perceived link between violence and the availability of guns, rather than on the link between violence and social-structure variables, including racism, religious hatred, poverty and gender inequality.

Soon after the horror in Montreal, the federal government convened a special task force to consider gun control. In 1993, a bill came into effect calling for screening of all applicants for a gun certificate. Some critics, who wanted tougher controls, called it a token law; some belittled the bill because, they claimed, it wouldn't prevent more guns from getting into Canadian hands. The critics were right in calling the legislation tokenism; but the current laws are tokens because they do not deal with the potential triggers of violence in the inequities of Canadian society.

It is estimated that registration of all guns in Canada is likely to cost the federal government up to $400 million, just as the government is cutting back more and more social programs. This money could be better spent targeting rampant poverty; it could be used to help alienated youths who abuse drugs and alcohol and commit most of the nation's murders, and to consider more constructive ways of overcoming the lack of employment opportunities. And it could go to help battered women find ways of safely leaving their abusive husbands.

III

Guns are misunderstood because violence is misunderstood. Typically, the human biological potential to inflict harm is vastly underestimated. Those who wish to ban guns in order to quell violence rarely probe the inevitability of violence in a societal structure that accepts racism, homelessness, widespread destitution and lack of opportunities for minority-group advancement.

To continue to debate gun use without considering the violent potential in each individual, and the power of society to unleash that potential, is mere intellectual and political pretension.

Being human means attempting to carve out a personal identity, a boundary between the self and otherness. Establishing and defending this boundary creates conflict, from argument to intimidation, to threat, to war. It is therefore difficult to imagine a world without weapons. Given its history, it is also difficult to imagine a United States without guns at the bedside, gunshots in the streets and guns worshipped in the culture. It is not often recognized that the effort to control a culturally entrenched service tool such as the gun will have to involve an effort to change deep social patterns and fundamental human wiring. Human biology, however, does not change quickly.

Humans are evolutionary newcomers, primitives who use primitive tools of destruction, including guns. It is consistent with human history to develop new weapons. Once, the bow and arrow was the world's main killing tool; and, indeed, some conclude that more deaths have been caused by arrows than by bullets.

When the gun goes the way of the bow and arrow—and it will—it will be because it has been superseded by new, more effective killing tools. Perhaps there will be electronic weapons to change or destroy brain function; they might be directed by computer or wireless palm-held telephones. Perhaps there will be near-undetectable pharmaceutical sprays that attack the nervous system or stop the heart.

As we shall see in the next chapter, in the gun culture, totalitarian control is the recipe for failure to control violence. Such failure itself becomes the excuse for every form of violence that can be conceivably unleashed against anyone who doesn't toe the mainstream line.

9

Rush to Vengeance:

A Consequence of the "Free Will" Society

"Jose Manuel Miguel Xavier Gonzalez, in a few short weeks, it will be spring. The snows of winter will float away, the ice will vanish, the air will become soft and balmy.

"In short, Jose Manuel Miguel Xavier Gonzalez, the annual miracle of the years will awaken and come to pass.

"But you won't be there.

"The rivers will run their soaring coarse to the sea, the timid desert flowers will put forth their tender shoots, the glorious valleys of this imperial domain will blossom as the rose.

"Still, you won't be there to see.

"From every treetop, some wild woods songster will carol his mating song, butterflies will sport in the sunshine, the busy bee will hum happy as it pursues its accustomed vocation, the gentle breeze will tease the tassels of the wild grasses—and all nature, Jose Manuel Miguel Xavier Gonzalez, will be glad but you.

"You won't be there to enjoy it because I command the sheriff of the county to lead you away to some remote spot, swing you by the neck from a knotting bough of some sturdy oak, and let you hang until you are dead.

"And then, Jose Manuel Miguel Xavier Gonzalez, I further command that such officer retire quickly from your dangling corpse, that vultures may descend from the heavens upon your filthy body until nothing shall remain but barren bleached bones of a cold-blooded, bloodthirsty, throat-cutting, sheep-herding, murdering son of a bitch."

—JUDGE ROY BEAN, TEXAS, 1881

I

Many residents of Union, South Carolina, would have cheered loudly had a modern-day Roy Bean sentenced Susan Smith to death for the murders of her sons, two-year-old Michael and fourteen-month-old Alex. To the great disappointment of many of her neighbors, and her ex-husband, Susan Smith will live to see the "annual miracle," albeit from a prison cell.

On October 25, 1994, after serving them pizza, Susan Smith strapped Michael and Alex into their car seats and rolled her Mazda into the dirty waters of John D. Long Lake. The car and its young passengers disappeared in six minutes.

She then made up an extraordinary story that made national headlines, claiming that a black man had snatched her car and sons. The police became increasingly suspicious. Smith finally read the signs and, after praying with the local sheriff, confessed her crime on November 3.

State psychiatrists declared her competent to stand trial, but described her as extremely fragile, and warned that her emotional instability might have numbed her during the commission of the crime. The defense, declaring Smith to be damaged, documented her long history of depression and suicide attempts. It also emphasized her sexual abuse at the hands of her stepfather, reportedly a "respected leader" of the Christian Coalition.

The continuation of this sexual relationship until just months before the murders, it was suggested, had contributed to her loss of self-esteem and her depression. Other sexual affairs, engaged in over a short period of time, further reflected her deep despair and growing desperation.

The prosecution portrayed Susan Smith as a promiscuous schemer, dismissing her difficult family history as "the abuse excuse."

In July 1995, the jury convicted Smith, but it also concluded that Smith was a "disturbed" person and that condemning her to death wouldn't serve justice. Instead, it condemned her to life. Smith will serve thirty years in prison before she is eligible for parole.

So the vultures awaiting Susan Smith's flesh must wait for another chance, but they need not fear going hungry.

Consider Varnall Weeks, who died in the electric chair in Alabama in May 1995. He had murdered a college student in 1981. Though Weeks had been diagnosed as a delusional paranoid-schizophrenic who believed that he would return to life as a giant flying tortoise controlling the universe, the Alabama court system concluded that he was sane enough to execute. Its decision was sustained by the U.S. Supreme Court, the institution which had ruled in 1986 that executing a mentally incompetent prisoner is cruel and unusual punishment.

More than a century after the hanging of Jose Manuel Miguel Xavier Gonzalez, Roy Bean is a popular fellow: Americans are clamoring for the death penalty. Many want even those killers judged to be insane to die, and dangerous criminals to be locked away forever.

Americans are out for vengeance, even though it does next to nothing to reduce violence and crime, and a great deal to encourage experimentation with totalitarian social policies.

Ironically, this hunger for vengeance comes at a time when science is revealing that violence is a human ingredient triggered by a variety of stimuli, not a disease to be cured or a moral failing to be rectified. To rid ourselves of violence would necessitate a rise above our evolutionary endowment and cultural history. For science is also challenging conventional thinking that humans are capable of being free agents who control their decisions and actions.

The Roy Bean America of today is enslaved to a desire to punish and is fueled by fear.

In Maricopa County, Arizona, 1,100 prisoners serving up to one year for misdemeanor offenses live under canvas in "Tent City" outside Phoenix. The temperature reaches 140F in summer and drops below freezing in winter. There is no adequate shelter. No counseling. No recreation. No education. There is nothing constructive to do. Not even lip-service is paid to rehabilitation. The goal is simple: make 'em pay.

In other jurisdictions, elected officials responding to the public's demand to punish are cutting back or eliminating television and sports in jails. Gone are weight rooms, tennis and basketball courts. Gone are pin-ups and pornography. Chain gangs and striped uniforms are back.

So is lock-'em-up-and-throw-away-the-key sentencing. A new federal crime bill hopes to add 100,000 police and many prisons across the United States. The most notable of the new sentencing laws is "three strikes," passed by California in March 1994. Under it, anyone convicted of a third major crime, referred to as a "felony," is sentenced to a minimum of twenty-five years, ostensibly to get drug users, violent thieves and murderers off the streets. However, a study of the law's first year shows that, of the 7,400 individuals charged, 70 percent had committed *non-violent* crimes. Moreover, "three strikes" places the court system under great strain, as those charged are increasingly likely to plead not guilty. (In 1996, California amended the law, allowing judges to show leniency in some cases—if the crime is not violent, or if the person charged has not been in prison for at least five years.)

Black Americans, to no one's surprise, receive a disproportionate number of "three strikes" convictions. (A California study showed that 57 percent of those given the lock-'em-up-for-good sentence were black, even though blacks are defendants in about 30 percent of felony prosecutions and make up 12 percent of the population.) This is in keeping with the trend: about 75 percent of new admissions to prisons are black or Hispanic. If the trend continues, more than half of black American males between the ages of eighteen and forty are likely to have been in some prison or other by the year 2010.

This is also a time of being jail-tough on drugs. In some jurisdictions, individuals who have no prior criminal record or history of drug use or of violent behavior are given mandatory sentences of ten years for possession. Department of Justice statistics reveal that drug offenders in state custody rose from 8 percent of the prison population in 1980 to 26 percent in 1993. In federal prisons, the figures for the same period rose from 25 percent to 60 percent. Yet the same statistics indicate that about 42 percent of those imprisoned on drug convictions either were messengers or played peripheral roles in drug-distribution networks.

Many critics of the "war on drugs," including a recently dismissed surgeon general, have suggested that legalizing drugs would end criminal involvement and be far more effective than the policing of the drug networks, which has been a dismal failure. The drop in drug convictions would allow the overcrowded prison system to be down-sized, as no more than a small number of petty drug users or distrib-utors go on to engage in violent crimes.

Instead, however, a fearful populace and political opportunism have combined merely to try to clear the streets of anyone who breaks the drug laws. It should therefore come as no surprise that the United States takes the gold medal as the world's premier jailer. The major-ity of Americans view the incarceration of some 1.5 million of their number—about 455 inmates for every 100,000 of population—as a proud achievement. South Africa wins the silver medal, with a rate of 311. Canada is in the pack at 111. Denmark, Japan and India straggle behind, with respective rates of 71, 42 and 34.

At any given time, 3.5 million Americans are on probation or parole. Should the trend continue—and there is no reason to expect it will not—the number of Americans under the control of the crim-inal-justice system may, in the next decade, exceed the 7.3-million population of New York City.

What is the $20-billion annual tab for prison construction and inmate maintenance buying? Some peace of mind for the fear-gripped populace who spend an additional $65 billion annually for private security firms and systems. It brings votes to politicians who stir public fears about vio-lent crime, and provides story lines for the media about how both the public and the politicians are reacting to threats of crime and violence.

What it is not buying in most jurisdictions is a reduction in violent crime. Survey results, of course, depend on a wide range of method-ologies for gathering, interpreting and reporting *available* data; but overall, statistics on rates of violent crime today are more or less the same as those documented in the 1970s and 1980s.

There is, predictably, a tendency among criminal-justice agencies to claim credit for any downturn in crime and violence. When, for example, New York City experienced a decline in homicide (down from 2,245 in 1990 to fewer than 1,000 in 1996), and a sharp drop in burglaries and robberies, compared with the previous year, police advanced the theory that more arrests, more preventive policing and more gun confiscations were the cause. A competing theory suggests the city's population is aging—and is therefore probably less violent.

Lest we relent on law and order, however, criminologists predict growth in the number of potentially more violent teenagers in the near future, which might well turn the statistics around. The additional 500,000 young males between the ages of fourteen and seventeen will likely significantly change the demographic—and violence—picture by the year 2000.

Whatever the reasons for sudden short-term drops or surges in violent crime, the longer-term statistics tell an important tale: the overall rate of violent crime is stable; therefore, the orgy of prison-building in the United States, which began in the early 1980s, and the doubling of the prison population have done nothing to create a safer society.

Canada, too, is succumbing to vengeance, even though its overall violent-crime rate has also remained stable for decades. (Since 1990, there has actually been a modest decline in crime and murder, but this may well be a temporary shift for demographic reasons, as is probably the case in the United States.) Canada—like most nations—has an appreciably lower rate of violent crime than the United States. Since the 1970s, for example, Canadian homicide rates have fluctuated between 2 and 3 per 100,000 population; the U.S. figure is about 9. The Canadian robbery rate is 121 per 100,000, roughly one-fifth the American rate.

Although the experts repeatedly tell Canadians they are not in a violent-crime crisis, polls show that about 25 percent of citizens believe they are surrounded by violence. This fear, probably exacerbated by strident coverage of crime in the Canadian media and by media access to U.S. reports of murder and mayhem, is translating into demands for harsher punishments, longer incarceration, and even a revival of the death penalty, which was abolished in 1976.

To date, however, apart from threatening to find legal ways to detain "dangerous" criminals beyond their sentences, Canadian legislators have yet to propose long-term sentencing schemes like those that characterize the U.S. criminal-justice system.

In response to the demands for harsher punishment and the likely shift of prison management to the private sector, film director Stuart Gordon has envisioned a future prison system that might even have given Judge Roy Bean pause. In Gordon's movie *Fortress*, prisoners are given microchip stomach implants called "intestinates" that produce severe pain when rules or orders are disobeyed. Laser beams replace cell bars, a computer tracks prisoners' waking thoughts and dreams, and a special chamber can erase their memories. The round-the-clock guards are half-human "enhancers" who require neither food nor sleep. Gordon's view is a logical extension of a prison system that has given up all pretense of offering rehabilitation.

The technology portrayed in *Fortress* is not yet with us, but embryonic elements of it are in use, and more are under development. The most common control system involves a small signal pack, or transponder, worn by an inmate under so-called house arrest. When the inmate leaves home, an alarm is set off. (This concept is similar to the shock an invisible electronic fence delivers when a pet tries to leave the property.)

In the future, it is likely that such "open" prisons will be common for low-risk inmates, who will be restricted to specific locations and travel routes in cities. Should an inmate break the rules (say, a pedophile goes near a school), a signal could alert police and/or an electronic relay could trigger drugs implanted in the arm—perhaps a sedative that will immobilize the individual until the police arrive.

For higher-risk criminals, more confinement and more powerful techniques to neutralize their undesirable behavior are likely to be developed.

II

We may know that locking people up is no meaningful solution to violence, but until recently there has been little action on the alternatives. One new approach, which is gaining some favor, comes from those who view violence as a "public health" problem; its advocates believe that violence, like an infectious disease, can be tracked and treated.

One spokesman for this movement is Mark Rosenberg, an epidemiologist at the Centers for Disease Control and Prevention in Atlanta. In a 1993 article in *Mother Jones* he states that he would like violence to be perceived as an *illness*, not as a matter for the criminal-justice system. If violence is recognized as an illness, Rosenberg argues, it can then potentially be prevented. Sounds good, but Rosenberg is not claiming that violence is a disease of society. No, it is an illness contracted by individuals.

First, says Rosenberg, we must discover patterns behind such violent behavior as homicide and suicide, and then attack with all the artillery of medicine and its allied professions. This could involve identifying, and then counseling, children who become emotionally numbed by violence around them and accept it as normal; it could involve introducing special programs to teach high-risk children anger control and conflict resolution, or setting up metal detectors to keep guns out of schools.

Rather than ignoring individuals at high risk for violence until they get scooped up by the prison system, striking early and often could give them alternatives to crime and violence.

One high-profile violence-prevention program has been created by Harvard University public-health specialist Deborah Prothrow-Stith. Called the "Violence Prevention Curriculum for Adolescents," it is being used in more than 5,000 U.S. schools. It teaches children how to recognize their psychological and physiological signs of anger, and demonstrates techniques they can use to calm themselves, thereby avoiding the conflict that can result in injury or death.

Prothrow-Stith shares Rosenberg's strong conviction that collaborative professional and grass-roots educational, mental-health and community services can be highly effective in turning some lives around.

While Prothrow-Stith and Rosenberg emphasize psychosocial approaches, another public-health advocate, criminologist Ray Jeffrey of Florida State University, concentrates on recognizing the biological factors that contribute to violence and preventing them from getting out of control. Jeffrey holds that the criminal-justice system ignores crime and violence that are the result of bad environments.

Jeffrey looks to neuroscience for more understanding of the deep insults inflicted on individuals by their experience. He refers, for example, to studies that show that violent individuals suffer a high rate of brain damage—from accidents, child abuse or drug abuse. He points out that damage to the brain's prefrontal lobes, for example, can disrupt the brain's organization with regard to rational and emotional behaviors, making it difficult for some individuals to respond appropriately to challenges in their environment.

Jeffrey rightly considers it professional negligence, if not malice, to exclude biological influences from any attempt to determine how violent behavior can be prevented. For instance, he points out that little medical attention is focused on how malnutrition may contribute to violent behavior, despite scientific evidence that associates brain chemicals—for which food provides the building-blocks—and states of awareness and moods. As we've already seen, a low supply of the food source tryptophan is correlated with violence.

Jeffrey contends that much research is required before a new and better science of criminology—one that marries biological and environmental dimensions—can provide more reliable insights into violent behavior and its prevention. Today the knowledge that such a connection does exist is overlooked in favor of punishment.

To speed things along, Jeffrey would like billions of dollars diverted from building new prisons to the creation of community-based programs to detect and address, via medical treatment or counseling, early brain damage and behavioral problems, child abuse, and nutritional disorders. He also advocates more prenatal and postnatal programs, as well as the decontamination of environments, removing such potentially neurotoxic substances as lead and aluminum. In sum, the pollution of the brains and bodies of children must stop, and communities must be redesigned if violence is to be controlled.

According to Jeffrey, once an arrest is made, particularly of a person with a record of violent crimes, every effort should be made to establish whether biological factors may be predisposing that individual to violence. Is there brain damage, perhaps due to early physical abuse? Brain scans might reveal it. Prescription-drug treatment may be appropriate. Is there malnutrition, perhaps due to poverty? A detailed nutrition history might be attempted, and diet corrected. If there is drug addiction, jail is hardly a rehabilitation center. And so on.

Jeffrey contends that some institutions are created to treat the physically ill, others to treat the mentally ill, but when chronically violent individuals (who are, after all, responsible for most violent crimes) are hauled off to prison, their overall health is ignored. Their behavior, the product of a wide range of social and biological influences, is likely to be attributed to immorality or viciousness. Punishment replaces treatment; vengeance substitutes for common sense. The prison system is no substitute for proper medical care and programs to prevent acts of violence

Jeffrey is right, as far as he goes; however, the public-health approach to violence is incomplete, as it does not address the social conditions—widespread poverty and racism—that help to trigger violence.

Peter Breggin, a Maryland psychiatrist, condemns the public-health approach for undercutting the attention that he believes should be focused on the white racism that contributes to the impoverishment, joblessness and desperation of the U.S. inner cities. He finds it difficult to fathom how violence, which is often a response to humiliating daily abuse, can so cavalierly be dismissed as an *illness* that can respond to prevention and treatment. He views with great suspicion superficial biomedical meddling in the lives of the oppressed and dispossessed.

Breggin has good reason to be suspicious. History is replete with examples of elites using biomedical policy to control, humiliate or destroy individuals or groups: we need to look no farther than the Holocaust and eugenics movements in Europe and North America.

Breggin, like some sociologists, emphasizes the need to include in any attempt to deal with crime and violence the context of economic interests and social class. In other words, although changing society's economic structure would enable individuals to compete more effectively, and thereby to have more life choices, the white ruling class narrows or shuts down the avenues of competition. It then labels the behavioral patterns that emerge in response to poverty and degradation as deviant, and builds prisons to keep its population safe from undesirable behavior.

In Breggin's view, the psychosocial goals of Rosenberg and Prothrow-Stith are little more than apologist Band-Aids; and the more medically oriented intervention schemes proposed by Jeffrey address biological damage but not the social inequalities that produce it.

This critique of the public-health approach to violence, despite its considerable merits, however, leaves some business unfinished. Given today's growing understanding of the brain, the important role of biology in violence cannot be dismissed; and it is difficult to speak of biology without considering our evolutionary heritage. This means that we recognize that there is "wiring" in the newborn brain that will produce culture and, in turn, will be influenced by culture. Neither the public-health approach to violence nor Breggin's adequately addresses this important concept.

Coming to terms with our evolutionary past means accepting that behavior is the product of more than solely social forces. The brain, which causes behavior, including violence, is principally an artifact of natural selection. Human aggression is a *genetically wired propensity* necessary for self-defense and survival. In other words, *it is normal to be aggressive*. However, evolution has also provided the brain, particularly the neocortex, with mechanisms to constrain aggressive impulses. Violence can still be triggered, however, depending on the neurochemical state of the brain; the behavior of other individuals; and social circumstances, including physical threat, humiliation and racist attack.

Many of those who intellectually accept Darwin's theory of evolution have difficulty accepting the full emotional and moral implications of such an argument. For if human life is framed by Darwinian evolution and the response of the environment to biological propensities, ultimately all our choices and decisions—our desires, belief systems and feelings—are the intimate dialogue of environment and brain, a process that shapes *all* behavior. Questions arise as to when, if ever, an individual is responsible for his or her actions.

A more flattering conception of humanity proposes that we are all capable of exercising free will, and therefore are responsible for our choices. This vision of free will, however, is increasingly being questioned, especially as neuroscience investigates how billions of nerve cells and their electrical and chemical constituents—not some entity known as "mind"—act in a highly complex processing of sensory data to produce consciousness.

Nonetheless, however, the free-will vision prevails in daily life: society rewards and punishes individuals on the principle that humans can control their actions. This is particularly evident in the court system, which insists that individuals are able to override their intentions, or "premeditation," if they so choose; those who break rules and laws are therefore to be held accountable. It is also believed that harsh punishment will deter not only further transgression by the convicted individual when he returns to society, but also the criminally-minded who are contemplating illegal activity.

The court absolves individuals of responsibility when they are judged to have been incapable of understanding the consequences of their actions or to have suffered from a diminished capacity to do so during the commission of the crime. (The latitude given by courts to defense arguments of insanity or temporary insanity varies. For example, under the stringent legal guidelines in South Carolina, Susan Smith was not allowed to plead that she was insane when she drowned her sons, despite the conclusion by state psychiatrists that she was likely mentally ill at the time.)

Yet, the courts are being pressed by defense lawyers to consider that their clients should be excused from responsibility, shifting blame to someone else, often one who has allegedly abused the accused. (Some of the better-known defenses have claimed that television incited murder, that feelings of rage due to racism provoked mass slaughter, and that being repeatedly abused by her husband prompted a woman to cut off his penis.)

Some reaction to "abuse excuse" arguments has been, predictably, hostile. There is concern that these cases undermine the credibility of the criminal-justice system. And indeed they do, although not in the way those opposed to them think. Abuse excuses, rather than being a threat to democracy, represent a reaction to a sadly outdated legal process.

For the real threat to humanity is societal vengeance, which can be seen as a form of eugenics, in which prison is a means to eliminate from society large sectors of the human population.

Vengeance renders individual lives worthless, as they can be eliminated from the culture.

III

Even those individuals who are appalled by the trend toward vengeance avoid facing up to the notion that humans may not be as responsible for their actions as we'd like to think. Consider the following statement in *The Real War on Crime*, issued by the National Criminal Justice Commission, a mix of private American citizens, including crime experts, community leaders and scholars, founded in 1994:

> The Commission members feel strongly that crime is an act of personal choice and that an effective criminal justice system holds individuals accountable for their criminal behavior. Nevertheless, those who wish to prevent crime before it occurs cannot ignore the fact that the majority of the people filling our prisons come from impoverished backgrounds and lack a formal education.

The commission statement then refers to well-documented research, showing that a "disproportionate amount of violent street crime occurs in areas that have the lowest incomes and the most desperate living conditions." And it points to medical research that suggests "children who are malnourished are more apt to engage in high-risk behavior when they get older."

For the commission, it boils down to this:

> Poverty is not an excuse for crime, nor is crime the exclusive province of low-income persons. But overall, countries with the highest ratio of poverty have the highest rates of crime. The same correlation holds for cities. It does not follow that an increase in poverty will translate immediately into an increase in crime. It does strongly imply that if overall poverty is reduced, then in the long run the amount of street crime associated with poverty will be reduced as well.

Elsewhere in its report, the commission has this to say about the cycle of violence:

The cycle of violence that begins in the home tends to reach beyond the home as the children grow older. Many become abusive toward their own partners and violent toward people in general. One study found that children growing up in homes where violence occurred were five times more likely to be delinquent or unmanageable than those not subjected to family violence.

Virtually all children living in a home where one parent assaults and terrorizes the other are aware of violence. Children from violent homes are almost two times more likely to commit crimes against other people and twenty-four times more likely to commit sexual assault crimes than their counterparts from nonviolent homes. They are also six times more likely to commit suicide.

The commission's report also focuses on how violence is learned early in life and on the fact that impoverished conditions are strongly associated with violent crime. Yet the logical question—how independent are people of their upbringing and environments?—the commission does not satisfactorily address. They seem to be telling us that social backgrounds matter, but apparently they don't matter enough. Where, then, do we draw the line on individual responsibility, as opposed to *social* responsibility?

One of the few who have dared to address this question systematically is the philosopher Patricia Churchland, of the Salk Institute and the University of San Diego, in La Jolla, California. She allows that much of daily life runs on the engine of personal responsibility; she concedes that we are a social species and, much like that of other mammals whose survival depends on cooperation and stability, our brain circuitry predisposes us toward social order.

Churchland, however, finds that there is little persuasive philosophical argument for the given that there is such an element as free will or "uncaused choice." Rather, citing philosopher David Hume, who viewed choice as something caused by desires, preferences and feelings, she argues that, logically, all behavior requires precipitating events, whether or not they are consciously perceived; behaviors therefore must be caused. It is also Hume who reminds us that people are usually considered responsible for their actions because of precipitating internal events—namely, their desires, preferences and feelings.

Churchland points out that neuroscience is showing that a person's internal or emotional life, a product of his or her interaction with social surroundings, is important in making choices: damage to the amygdala and other brain structures may lead to a lack of emotional response and bizarre behavior; an individual with an intact brain may make more socially appropriate decisions, having internalized correctly the cognitive and emotional cues.

The implication here is that there is no free will, only the highly individualized internalization of, and reaction to, social cues, some of which society deems more appropriate than others.

Even though Churchland is aware of the profound legal and social-policy questions this view raises, she then takes the practical road, concluding that social order is a necessity, and deeming it wise to continue the practice of holding individuals responsible for their actions.

Churchland is correct; this is, for now, the *only* road we can travel without social chaos. We continue, however, to speed along this practical road without the necessary wisdom to minimize its dangers. Consequently we are likely to face an escalation of vengeance, more violence, ultimately widescale social conflict in both poor and rich nations, and probably even the destruction of life on this planet.

10

Primitive Planet:

The Rough Road Ahead

I

Images of a future ruled by violence are commonly found in fiction, particularly science fiction. Take a macabre Japanese animation video series featuring a giant warrior known as "Violence Jack." It portrays a world destroyed by natural disasters, where the survivors fight disease and starvation and join warring factions; only the most brutish will survive.

It is easy to dismiss such notions as fanciful artistic preoccupations; after all, art always experiments with the boundaries of the possible. Violence Jack's world of bedlam and extreme violence, however, may be yet another example of fiction becoming fact.

Do we overestimate our potential to survive on this planet?

Beneath the veneer of civilization are powerful animal energies that sometimes cannot be controlled; we are still not accustomed to thinking of social stability as a powerful glue that usually keeps us from enacting our full potential for violence. As environments degrade, and as social structures decline in their ability to heal divisions among peoples, that potential is more likely to be unleashed.

Social pundits often contend that our species has evolved sufficiently to enable societal institutions to protect us from oblivion.

This is really a leap of faith, because it ignores the potential of people everywhere on this planet to break down under severe stress.

Under the appearance of stability in developed nations is a widening gap between rich and poor. One result is the broadening base of impoverished, jobless, alienated and frustrated men and women. One common mistake is to view rich nations as having mere "pockets" of poverty in the midst of plenty. But a more realistic evaluation of life in, for example, the United States reveals that some of these supposedly isolated "pockets," robbed of employment opportunities and adequate social supports, including health care, have become alternative cultures, breeding-grounds for violence in the day-to-day struggle for mere survival. One price we already pay for this widespread underclass culture is a violent drug trade that has helped to destabilize socially the wealthiest and most powerful nation on Earth.

Moreover, many developed nations have large and increasing numbers of poor children; the United States has some of the poorest; in Canada, 20 percent of children—about 1.4 million—are poor, an increase of about 0.5 million from a decade ago. These children are more at risk for illness, accidental death and *violent behavior*, as they, like their elders, believe that they must use *ingenuity* (often another word for "crime") to survive.

The developed world is likely to be further destabilized by crises in poor nations. As one example, social pundit Robert Kaplan, writing in *The Atlantic Monthly*, concluded on the basis of his research in West Africa that the developing world is on the brink of environmental collapse, and that, as renewable resources become increasingly scarce, the resulting anarchy will spread to the developed world. It is highly likely, he argues, that competition for such commodities as land and water will continue to provoke widespread social conflict.

Thomas Homer-Dixon, a professor of political science at the University of Toronto, shares elements of Kaplan's apocalyptic vision. In a 1991 article in the journal *International Security*, he linked environmental decay to social conflict, and helped re-energize the long-standing debate on our ability to survive on this planet. Homer-Dixon argues that environmental destruction may be irreversible in many parts of the developing world; it may be too late, in some cases, to turn conditions around, with even the most enlightened social/political changes to encourage environmental reform. He also concludes that "entire countries can now be deforested in a few decades, most of a region's topsoil can disappear in a generation, and acute ozone depletion may take place in as few as 20 years." For example, he cites China's arable land as being seriously in decline and concludes that India, with a projected population of 1.5 billion by 2025, will find it difficult, if not impossible, during the next century to adapt to rapidly declining water levels and its shrinking natural resources.

Homer-Dixon also warns that the ability of nations to adapt to crises may itself be blocked by unstable political conditions.

He sums up the world's plight this way:

> Think of a stretch limo in the potholed streets of New York City,
> where homeless beggars live. Inside the limo are the air-conditioned
> post-industrial regions of North America, Europe, the emerging
> Pacific Rim and a few other isolated places, with their trade summitry
> and computer-information highways. Outside is the rest of mankind,
> going in a completely different direction.

Not everyone, of course, agrees. The optimists can usually find indicators—higher incomes, literacy rates and life-expectancy, for example—that life on Earth is improving. Homer-Dixon rightly counters that their analyses rely too heavily on rapid economic growth as a means of keeping the world socially secure. The optimists also like to pile up statistics that reveal the average numbers of people in many countries who are benefiting from, say, health care and food production. This approach conceals more than it reveals—namely, the problematic environmental, social and political trends certain nations are experiencing.

Some of the optimists believe that new information technologies such as the Internet will help foster significant social and economic change. Instant communication, they say, will empower the disenfranchised; the "Net" will offer more roadmaps to the future, and, in turn, this will enable us to build a more democratic world. There is, however, not much, if any, evidence to back such enthusiasm. At a 1996 conference in Washington, D.C., sponsored by the World Future Society, various speakers pointed out that, thus far, the new information technology has cost millions of people their jobs and is helping to establish a wider gap between rich and poor; the Net, they argued, is an outgrowth of a global economy, and it is consolidating the power of a small "technocratic elite" that will control "ByteCity." One conference speaker noted that two-thirds of the people on Earth have never even used a telephone.

The Net may also make it more difficult to envision social change; a glut of infotainment may gradually jam critical/political thinking. In the Information Age, commercial interests are likely to set the daily agenda for the "wired."

One potential consequence of social and/or environmental breakdown and the violence it unleashes is totalitarianism. When nations approach the breaking point, they tend to resort to primitive, fascistic controls.

The developed nations are responding to social tensions by getting tougher with "losers": there are repeated calls for jailing criminals for long terms, even for petty drug crimes, and for throwing away the key should violence be involved. Losers are blamed for lacking moral fiber and not trying hard enough to become winners. Such underlying causes as impoverished environments that breed discontent and violence are ignored. This mind-set is likely to further encourage politicians to campaign, on behalf of fearful constituents, for reduced freedoms, including censorship of television programming and other forms of news and entertainment that are said to provoke violent and other "unsuitable" forms of behavior.

Complicating matters further, particularly in the United States, are religious movements that are entering the political mainstream. With simple-minded, holier-than-thou moral-reformism (sometimes referring enthusiastically to traditional ways as "virtues") making powerful inroads, more individuals are likely to become targets of control. This will only add to "them" and "us" tensions.

The get-tough approach has escalated in the developing world as governments use strong-arm, murderous tactics to control their populations. These "praetorian" or "hard regimes," as Homer-Dixon calls them, stoke further conflict and, consequently, prevent a rational response to complex environmental problems and their violent consequences.

Yet, Homer-Dixon himself reveals a glimmer of guarded optimism as he allows that global cooperation just might help some nations avert social chaos, if rich and poor nations can find ways to redistribute wealth, control population and renew scarce resources.

How likely is this hopeful scenario in light of past performance?

As things stand, not very, considering that the *developed* nations, which must figure largely in any widescale rescue mission, are increasingly vulnerable to social upheaval and violence in ways that are not being addressed.

Over the longer term, however, as the economic repercussions of social chaos in the developing world impinge on vulnerable social "environments" in developed, so-called democratic nations, it may become increasingly difficult for even these governments to keep the lid on widespread violence without resorting to murderous, hard-regime tactics.

II

Is it possible, then, to minimize the dangers on the rough road ahead?

This is a question premised on hope—hope that we can develop effective strategies to save ourselves from widespread violence and destruction.

It may be prudent, however, to assume the worst and not underestimate the potential for social upheaval in both the developing and the developed world.

As far as natural disasters are concerned, there is obviously very little we can do, at least at present. If earthquakes or other forces were to level our cities our potential for violence would quickly become evident. The science-fiction writers are dead on when they assume life anywhere on Earth after an environmental cataclysm would be hellish and brutish.

What can be done to minimize the environmental destruction that Kaplan and Homer-Dixon link to social chaos? Perhaps some assembly of nations will emerge in the interests of global survival and chart an effective plan to achieve a sustaining environment. Individuals might also campaign strongly for intervention and adopt environmentally friendly behaviors that *might* contribute to making a difference over the long term. But there are limits to what individuals with a strong personal commitment to behavioral change can do in the midst of many who will not so commit.

The same goes for trying to live more compassionately in the face of pressures to fend for oneself. Yes, we can try to be more understanding of the dilemmas others face; we can be more forgiving of the crimes others commit; we can even raise our voices against a prison system that warehouses huge numbers of people whose chances to benefit from the promise of "rapid economic growth" were minimal at the outset; and we can support social programs that generate jobs and distribute society's wealth more widely.

Perhaps such an expenditure of energy will enable us at least to look into the mirror in the morning and see that we have tried to make a difference.

My hope for better days rests with the power of ideas to "move mountains" by transforming opinion and behavior. I base this hope on the evidence showing how social inputs from a very early age make a powerful mark on the brain. It is my further hope that the scope of these inputs will change over time and that new generations will develop brains that enhance the human potential for cooperation.

One big battle ahead will be to keep our minds open to new ideas, and to avoid being overwhelmed by commercial messages that homogenize culture and give rise to mind control.

Though always hopeful—I believe the human capacity to think abstractly promotes hope—I also believe our world is fast reaching the breaking point, the point of no return, a state where violence will swell everywhere, making us more and more vulnerable to the forces of extinction.

We are, after all, essentially primitives living on a primitive planet, fighting for our stake in a universe of great mystery. Some of us will probably escape to the stars, where life with its potential for both cooperation and violence will begin anew.

Last Word

Writing this book was both depressing and liberating. While it required that I come to terms with my animal origins and face up to my own potential for violence, it made me better appreciate that long and wondrous evolutionary road we travel on this tiny planet in an ocean of stars.

At first it was difficult to think of myself as having a powerful potential for violence, as having machinery in my brain that could unleash violent behavior under a wide range of conditions, including illness and stressful living. I had to accept that my behavior is probably the result of a complex interactive process—the ongoing dialogue between brain and environment, mediated by the firing of neurons and the interplay of brain chemicals. I had to confront the probability that I was not free to choose, not the controller of my decisions or actions. I understand this intellectually; yet, because my brain produces consciousness and the illusion that I am a separate, thinking entity, I will doubtless behave as though I am the principal architect of my destiny.

Take the writing of this book. Why did I write it? I decided that the subject interested me? No, this book is the result of a vast progression of exchanges between my brain and my environment, at least since my birth (and likely since my conception). It has nothing to do with some central command-post in my brain that I like to refer to as "the mind." What you are now reading is the essence of who I am always in the process of becoming.

Looking at violence in this context should make it easier to appreciate why everyone is capable of causing harm or murder. We are the ever-changing products of complex, variable history. The extent to which each of us is violent is directly linked to our biological heritage and to the dynamic interaction between complex brain processes and a vast, ongoing array of social inputs. Writing or reading this book merely adds to the interchange.

Such thinking about oneself runs counter to the steady drumbeat of exhortations to take responsibility for one's actions. It runs counter to the idea that anyone—everyone—should be able to control violent feelings. It runs counter to the powerful insistence of organized religion that there is life beyond the physical and that there are rules we can follow to maximize our chances of living it. Finally, it highlights our evolved social priorities, which allow huge populations to live in poverty while suggesting that all people could, if they would only put their minds to it, become prosperous, constructive and content.

In writing this book, I feel that I have increased my understanding of the potent influences that shape people's lives, including their violent ways. It no longer bothers me that I may be "merely" an ongoing state of information exchange; that I am far from being a finished product, indeed, is liberating.

Bibliography

Books

American Medical Association. *Violence*. Chicago: American Medical Association, 1992

Andreasen, N.C. *The Broken Brain*. New York: Harper & Row, 1984

Ardrey, R. *The Territorial Imperative*. London: Property and Nations, 1966

Arendt, H. *Eichmann in Jerusalem*. Harmondsworth: Penguin, 1953

Asimov, I. *The Human Brain*. New York: Plume, 1963

Babuta, S., and J. Bragard. *Evil*. London: Weidenfeld & Nicolson, 1985

Benedict, R. *Patterns Of Culture*. Boston: Houghton-Mifflin, 1934

Boas, F. *Anthropology and Modern Life*. New York: Dover, 1928

Breggin, P. R. M.D. *Talking Back to Prozac*. New York: St. Martin's, 1994

———. *Toxic Psychiatry*. New York: St. Martin's, 1991

Breggin, P.R., M.D., and G.R. Breggin. *The War against Children*. New York: St. Martin's, 1994

Brockman, J. *The Third Culture*. New York: Touchstone, 1995

Brodie, R. *Virus of the Mind*. Seattle: Integral, 1996

Churchland, P.S. *The Engine of Reason, the Seat of the Soul*. London: MIT Press, 1995

———. *Neurophilosophy*. Cambridge, Mass.: MIT Press, 1986

Churchland, P.S., and T. Sejnowski. *The Computational Brain*. Cambridge, Mass.: MIT Press, 1992

Cohen, D. *The Secret Language of the Mind*. San Francisco: Chronicle, 1996

Cornwell, J. *The Power to Harm*. New York: Viking, 1996

Crichton, M. *The Terminal Man*. New York: Knopf, 1972

Crick, F. *The Astonishing Hypothesis*. New York: Scribner's, 1994

Damasio, A.R. *Descartes' Error*. New York: Putnam, 1994

Darwin, C. *The Descent of Man, and Selection in Relation to Sex.* 1871; Harmondsmith: Penguin, 1968

———. *On the Origin of the Species.* 1859; Harmondsworth: Penguin, 1968

Dawkins, R. *River Out of Eden.* New York: Basic, 1995

———. *The Selfish Gene.* Oxford: Oxford University Press, 1976

Deats, S.M., and L.T. Lenker, eds. *The Aching Hearth.* New York: Plenum, 1991

Degler, C.N. *In Search of Human Nature.* Oxford: Oxford University Press, 1991

Dennett, D.C. *Consciousness Explained.* Boston: Little, Brown, 1991

———. *Darwin's Dangerous Idea.* New York: Simon & Schuster, 1995

Dershowitz, A.M. *The Abuse Excuse.* New York: Little, Brown, 1994

Descartes, R. *Discourse on Method.* Chicago: Paquin Printers, 1899

Devlin, Keith. *Goodbye, Descartes.* New York: Wiley, 1996

De Waal, F. *Good Natured.* Cambridge, Mass.: Harvard University Press, 1996

Diamond, J. *The Third Chimpanzee.* New York: HarperPerennial, 1992

Douglas, J., and M. Olshaker. *Mind Hunter.* New York: Scribner's, 1995

Dunnigan, J.F. *Digital Soldiers.* New York: St. Martin's, 1996

Edelman, M. *Bright Air, Brilliant Fire.* New York: Basic, 1992

Evans, R.I. *Konrad Lorenz: The Man and His Ideas.* New York: Harcourt Brace Jovanovich, 1975

Ewing, C.P. *Kids Who Kill.* New York: Avon, 1990

Falk, D. *Braindance.* New York: Holt, 1992

Fox, R. *The Challenge of Anthropology.* New Brunswick, N.J.: Transaction, 1994

Fromm, E. *The Anatomy of Human Destructiveness.* New York: Holt, 1973

———. *The Heart of Man.* New York: Harper & Row, 1964

———. *The Sane Society.* New York: Rinehart, 1955

Galton, F. *Hereditary Genius: An Enquiry into Its Laws and Consequences.* 1892; Cleveland: World Publishing, 1946

Gilder, G. *Life after Television.* New York: Norton, 1990

Goddard, H. *The Kallikak Family.* New York: Macmillan, 1912

Goldsmith, T.H. *The Biological Roots of Human Nature.* New York: Oxford University Press, 1991

Goodall, Jane. *The Chimpanzees of Gombe.* Cambridge, MA: Harvard University Press, 1986

———. *Through a Window.* Boston: Houghton-Mifflin, 1990

Gould, S.J. *Ever Since Darwin.* New York: Norton, 1973

Grossman, Lt.-Col. D. *On Killing.* New York: Little, Brown, 1995

Hubbard, R., and E. Wald. *Exploding the Gene Myth.* Boston: Beacon Press, 1993

Hume, David. *A Treatise on Human Nature.* 1738; London: Everyman's Library, 1956

Hunt, M. *The Story of Psychology.* New York: Doubleday, 1993

Itzin, C., ed. *Pornography.* Oxford: Oxford University Press, 1992

Jaynes, J. *The Origin of Consciousness in the Breakdown of the Bicameral Mind.* Boston: Houghton-Mifflin, 1976

Jencks, C. *Rethinking Social Policy.* Cambridge, Mass.: Harvard University Press, 1992

Kandel, E.R., J.H. Schwartz, and T.M. Jessell, eds. *Principles of Neural Science,* 3rd ed. New York: Elsevier Science, 1991

Kaplan, R. *The Ends of the Earth.* New York: Random House, 1966

Kotulak, R. *Inside the Brain*. Kansas City: Andrews & McMeel, 1996

Kramer, P.D. *Listening to Prozac*. New York: Viking, 1993

Kroker, A., and M.A. Wienstein. *Data Trash*. New York: St. Martin's, 1994

La Plante, E. *Seized*. New York: HarperCollins, 1993

LeDoux, J. *The Emotional Brain*. New York: Simon & Schuster, 1996

Levin, J., and J.A. Fox. *Mass Murder*. New York: Berkeley, 1985

Lewis, D.O., and D.A. Balla. *Delinquency and Psychopathology*. New York: Grune & Stratton, 1976

Lewis, J., and B. Towers. *Naked Ape or Homo Sapiens?* New York: Humanities, 1969

Lewontin, R.C. *Biology as Ideology*. New York: HarperCollins, 1991

Lombroso, C. *Crime—Its Causes and Remedies*. London: Horton, 1911

Lorenz, K. *On Aggression*. New York: Harcourt, Brace & World, 1963

Luria, A.R. *The Working Brain: An Introduction to Neuropsychology*. New York: Basic, 1973

MacKinnon, C.A. *Only Words*. Cambridge, Mass.: Harvard University Press, 1993

Mandar, J. *Four Arguments for the Elimination of Television*. New York: Quill, 1977

Mark, Vernon, and Frank Ervin. *Violence and the Brain*. New York: Harper & Row, 1970

Masters, B. *Killing for Company*. New York: Random House, 1993

McKibben, B. *The Age of Missing Information*. New York: Plume, 1992

Mednick, S.A., and K.O. Christiansen. *Biological Bases of Criminal Behavior*. New York: Gardner, 1977

Milgram, S. *Obedience to Authority*. New York: Random House, 1974

Mithen, S. *The Prehistory of the Mind*. London: Thames & Hudson, 1996

Mitroff I.I., and W. Bennis. *The Unreality Industry*. New York: Oxford University Press, 1989

Moir, A., and D. Jessel. *Brainsex*. London: Mandarin, 1989

Monod, J. *Chance and Necessity*. New York: Knopf, 1971

Montagu, A. *The Nature of Human Aggression*. New York: Oxford University Press, 1976

Morris, D. *The Naked Ape*. New York: Dell, 1967

National Research Council. *Understanding Child Abuse and Neglect*. Washington, D.C.: National Academy, 1993

National Research Council, A.J. Reiss, and J.A. Roth, eds. *Understanding and Preventing Violence*. Washington, D.C.: National Academy, 1993

Negroponte, N. *Being Digital*. New York: Knopf, 1995

Norris, J. *Serial Killers*. New York: Doubleday, 1988

——. *Walking Time Bombs*. New York: Bantam, 1992

Olsen, J. *The Misbegotten Son*. New York: Island, 1993

Ornstein, R., and P. Ehrlich. *New World, New Mind*. New York: Doubleday, 1989

Ornstein, R., and C. Swencionis, eds. *The Healing Brain*. New York: Guilford, 1990

Penfield, W. *The Mystery of the Mind*. Princeton, N.J.: Princeton University Press, 1975

Penrose, R. *Shadows of the Mind*. Oxford: Oxford University Press, 1994

——. *The Emperor's New Mind*. Oxford: Oxford University Press, 1989

Persinger, M.A. *Neuropsychological Bases of God Beliefs*. New York: Praeger, 1987

Pinkney, A. *The American Way of Violence*. New York: Random House, 1972

Postman, N. *Technopoly*. New York: Vintage, 1992

Postman, N., and S. Powers. *How to Watch TV News*. New York: Penguin, 1992

Prochiantz, A. *How the Brain Evolved.* New York: McGraw-Hill, 1989

Prothrow-Stith, D., M.D. *Deadly Consequences.* New York: HarperPerennial, 1991

Renfrew, C., and B.W. Zubrow, eds. *The Ancient Mind: Elements of Cognitive Archaeology.*

Regush, N., ed. *Visibles and Invisibles.* New York: Little, Brown, 1973

Restak, R., M.D. *Brainscapes.* New York: Hyperion, 1995

———. *Receptors.* New York: Bantam, 1993

———. *The Brain.* New York: Warner, 1979

———. *The Mind Has a Brain of Its Own.* New York: Crown, 1991

———. *The Modular Brain.* New York: Scribner's, 1994

Rheingold, H. *Virtual Reality.* New York: Summit, 1991

Scholder, A., ed. *Critical Condition.* San Francisco: City Lights, 1993

Scully, D. *Understanding Sexual Violence.* London: HarperCollins Academic, 1990

Searle, J. *Minds, Brains, and Science.* Cambridge, Mass.: Harvard University Press, 1984

———. *The Rediscovery of Mind.* London: MIT Press, 1992

Sherman, B., and P. Judkins. *Glimpses of Heaven, Visions of Hell.* London: Hodder & Stoughton, 1992

Shipman, P. *The Evolution of Racism.* New York: Simon & Schuster, 1994

Shukman, D. *The Sorcerer's Challenge.* London: Coronet, 1995

Silberman, C.E. *Criminal Violence, Criminal Justice.* New York: Vintage, 1978

Skinner, B.F. *Beyond Freedom and Dignity.* New York: Bantam, 1972

Slouka, M. *War of the Worlds: Cyberspace and the High-Tech Assault on Reality.* New York: Basic, 1995

Snell, B. *The Discovery of the Mind.* New York: Harper & Row, 1953

Stein, D.G., S. Brailowsky, and B. Will. *Brain Repair.* New York: Oxford University Press, 1995

Stock. G. *Metaman.* New York: Simon & Schuster, 1993

Storr, A. *Human Aggression.* New York: Atheneum, 1968

———. *Human Destructiveness.* New York: Routledge, 1991

Strean, Dr. H., and L. Freeman. *Our Wish to Kill.* New York: Avon, 1991

Sumner, W. *Folkways.* New York: Doubleday, 1906

Timberlake, J.H. *Prohibition and the Progressive Movement, 1900–1920.* New York: Atheneum, 1963

Time-Life Books. *Mass Murderers.* Alexandria, Va.: Time-Life Books, 1992

Tinbergen, N. *The Study of Instinct.* Oxford: The Clarendon Press, 1951

Valenstein, E.S. *Brain Control.* New York: Wiley, 1973

Vines, G. *Raging Hormones.* Berkeley: University of California Press, 1993

Watson, L. *Dark Nature.* London: Hodder & Stoughton, 1995

Wills, C. *The Runaway Brain.* New York: Basic, 1993

Wilson, C. *A Criminal History of Mankind.* London: Grafton, 1984

Wilson, E.O. *On Human Nature.* London: Harvard University Press, 1978

———. *Sociobiology.* Cambridge, MA: Harvard University Press, 1975

Wilson, W.J. *When Work Disappears.* New York: Knopf, 1996

Wrangham, R., and D. Peterson. *Demonic Males.* Boston: Houghton-Mifflin, 1996

Wright, R. *The Moral Animal.* New York: Pantheon, 1994

Articles

Anderson, Elijah. "The Code of the Streets." *The Atlantic Monthly*, May 1994

Beach, F. "The Descent of Instinct." *Psychological Review*, 62 (1955)

Blakeslee, S. "How the Brain Might Work: A New Theory of Consciousness." *The New York Times*, March 21, 1995

Blow, R. "A Social Disease." *Mother Jones*, May/June 1993

Breggin, P. "The Violence Initiative: A Racist Biomedical Program for Social Control." Center for the Study of Psychiatry, n.d.

Bridges, P.K., and J.R. Bartlett. "Psychosurgery: Yesterday and Today." *British Journal of Psychiatry* 131 (1977)

Cascardi, M., et al. "Marital Aggression." *Archives of Internal Medicine*, 152 (June 1992)

Centerwall, B.S. "Television and Violence." *Journal of the American Medical Association* 267/22 (June 1992)

Chalmers, D.J. "The Puzzle of Conscious Experience." *Scientific American*, December 1995

Chesler, P. "What Is Justice for a Rape Victim?" *On the Issues*, Winter 1996

Churchland, P.S. "Feeling Reasons." Draft copy (April 20, 1995)

Ciccone, J.R. "Murder, Insanity, and Medical Expert Witnesses." *Archives of Neurology* 49 (June 1992)

Conlogue, R. "Why Pornography Is a Myth." *The Globe and Mail*, January 4, 1994

Council on Scientific Affairs, American Medical Association. "Violence Against Women: Relevance for Medical Practitioners." *Journal of the American Medical Association* 267/23 (June 1992)

Crick, F., and C. Koch. "Towards a Neurobiological Theory of Consciousness." *Seminars in the Neurosciences*, 2 (1990)

Damasio, H., et al. "The Return of Phineas Gage." *Science*, 264 (1994)

Dart, R. "The Predatory Transition from Ape to Man." *International Anthropological and Linguistic Review*, 1 (1954)

Donaldson, J. "The Physiological Significance of Manganese in the Brain: Its Relation to Schizophrenia and Neurodegenerative Disorders." *Neurotoxicology* 8 (1987)

Dunn, K. "Just as Fierce." *Mother Jones*, November/December 1994

Eichelman, B. "Aggressive Behavior: From Laboratory to Clinic." *Archives of General Psychiatry* 49 (June 1992)

Elliot, F.A. "Violence." *Archives of Neurology* 49 (June 1992)

Feldman, Marilyn, et al. "Filicidal Abuse in the Histories of 15 Condemned Murderers." *Bulletin of the American Academy of Psychiatry* 14/4 (1986)

Ferris, C. "The Rage of Innocents." *The Sciences*, March/April 1996

Gibbs, W.W. "Seeking the Criminal Element." *Scientific American*, March 1995

Gottschalk, L.A., et al. "Abnormalities in Hair Trace Elements as Indicators of Aberrant Behavior." *Comprehensive Psychiatry* 32/3 (May/June 1991)

Grant, R. "Banging Up the Bad Guys." *The Independent on Sunday*, May 21, 1995

Grisham, J. "Natural Bred Killers." *The Sunday New York Times*, April 7, 1966

Harlow, H. "The Nature of Love." *American Psychologist*, 13 (1958)

Higley, J.D., et al. "Cerebrospinal Fluid Monoamine and Adrenal Correlates of Aggression in Free-Ranging Rhesus Monkeys." *Archives of General Psychiatry* 49 (June 1992)

Homer-Dixon, T.F. "Environmental Scarcities and Violent Conflict: Evidence form Cases." *International Security*, Fall 1991

———. "The Ingenuity Gap: Can Poor Countries Adapt to Resource Scarcity?" *Population and Development Review*, September 1995

———. "Is Anarchy Coming? A Response to the Optimists." *The Globe and Mail*, May 10, 1994

———. "On the Threshold: Environmental Changes as Causes of Acute Conflict." *International Security*, Summer 1994

Homer-Dixon, T.F., et al. "Environmental Change and Violent Conflict." *Scientific American*, February 1993

Horgan, J. "Fractured Functions: Does the Brain Have a Supreme Integrator?" *Scientific American*, December 1993

Hucker, S., et al. "Cerebral Damage and Dysfunction in Sexually Aggressive Men." *Annals of Sex Research* 1 (1988)

Hucker, S., et al. "Neuropsychological Impairment in Pedophiles." *Canadian Journal of Behavioral Science* 18/4 (1986)

Hucker, S. and L. Stermac. "The Evaluation and Treatment of Sexual Violence, Necrophilia, and Asphyxiophilia." *Psychiatric Clinics of North America* 15/3 (September 1992)

Jacobs, B.L. "Serotonin, Motor Activity and Depression-Related Disorders." *American Scientist* 82 (September/October 1994)

James, W. "What Is an Emotion?" *Mind*, 9 (1884)

Jenkins, P. "The Inner Darkness: Serial Murder and the Nature of Evil." *Chronicles*, January 1995

Kalin, N.H. "The Neurobiology of Fear." *Scientific American*, May 1993

Kaminer, W. "Second Thoughts on the Second Amendment." *The Atlantic Monthly*, March 1996

Kaplan, R. "The Coming Anarchy." *The Atlantic Monthly*, February 1994

Kimura, M., et al. "Effect of Subacute Manganese Feeding on Serotonin Metabolism in the Rat." *Journal of Toxicology and Environmental Health* 4 (1978)

Kingwell, M. "Meet Tad, the Doom-Meister." *Saturday Night*, September 1995

Kruesi, M.J.P., et al. "A 2-Year Prospective Follow-up Study of Children and Adolescents with Disruptive Behavior Disorders." *Archives of General Psychiatry* 49 (June 1992)

Langevin, R., et al. "Sexual Sadism: Brain, Blood, and Behavior." *Annals of the New York Academy of Sciences*, n.d.

Levay, S., and D.H. Hamer. "Evidence for a Biological Influence in Male Homosexuality." *Scientific American*, May 1994

Levy, E. "She Just Doesn't Understand: The Feminist Face-off on Pornographic Legislation." *On the Issues*, Fall 1993

Lewis, D.O. "From Abuse to Violence: Psychophysiological Consequences of Maltreatment." *Journal of the American Academy of Child and Adolescent Psychiatry* 31/3 (May 1992)

Lewis, D.O. and S.S. Shanok. "Medical Histories of Delinquent and Nondelinquent Children: An Epidemiological Study." *American Journal of Psychiatry* 134/9 (September 1977)

Lewis, D.O., et al. "Race Bias in the Diagnosis and Disposition of Violent Adolescents." *American Journal of Psychiatry* 137/10 (October 1980)

Lewis, D.O., et al. "Psychomotor Epilepsy and Violence in a Group of Incarcerated Adolescent Boys." *American Journal of Psychiatry* 139/7 (July 1982)

Lewis, D.O., et al. "Race, Health, and Delinquency." *Journal of the American Academy of Child Psychiatry* 24/2 (1985)

Lewis, D.O., et al. "Neuropsychiatric, Psychoeducational, and Family Characteristics of 14 Juveniles Condemned to Death in the United States." *American Journal of Psychiatry* 145/5 (May 1988)

Lewis, D.O., et al. "Toward a Theory of the Genesis of Violence: A Follow-up Study of Delinquents." *Journal of the American Academy of Child and Adolescent Psychiatry* 28/3 (1989)

Llinas, R., and U. Ribary. "Coherent 40Hz Oscillation Characterizes Dream State in Humans." *Proceedings of the National Academy of Sciences*, 90 (1993)

LoPiccolo, P. "Something Snapped." *Technology Review*, October 1996

McConaghy, N., "Are Sex Offenders Ever Cured?" *The Medical Journal of Australia* 162 (April 17, 1995)

McGoey, C.S., "When Regular Guys Rape: The Trial of the Glen Ridge Four." *On the Issues*, Fall 1993

Mifflin, L. "Advertisers Chase a New Target: 'Cybertots.'" *The New York Times*, March 29, 1996

Morand, C., et al. "Clinical Response of Aggressive Schizophrenics to Oral Tryptophan." *Biological Psychiatry* 18/5 (1983)

Moy, J.A., and M.R. Sanchez. "The Cutaneous Manifestations of Violence and Poverty." *Archives of Dermatology* 128 (June 1992)

Murphy, V.A., et al. "Elevation of Brain Manganese in Calcium Deficient Rats" *Neurotoxicology* 12 (1991)

Newberger, E.H., et al. "Abuse of Pregnant Women and Adverse Birth Outcome." *Journal of the American Medical Association* 267/17 (May 1992)

Oldenburg, A. "Suit Blames 'Killers' for Woman's Injuries." *USA Today*, July 10, 1996

Persinger, M.A. "Geophysical Variables and Behavior: LV. Predicting the Details of Visitor Experiences and the Personality of Experients: The Temporal-Lobe Factor." *Perceptual and Motor Skills* 68 (1989)

————. "Religious and Mystical Experiences as Artifacts of Temporal-Lobe Function: A General Hypothesis." 57 (1983)

————. "Sense of a Presence and Suicide Ideation Following Traumatic Brain Injury: Indications of Right-Hemispheric Intrusions from Neuropsychological Profiles." *Psychological Reports* 75 (1994)

————. "The Sensed Presence as Right-Hemispheric Intrusions into the Left-Hemispheric Awareness of Self: An Illustrative Case Study." *Perceptual and Motor Skills* 78 (1994)

————. "Vectorial Cerebral Hemisphericity as Differential Sources for the Sensed Presence, Mystical Experiences and Religious Conversions." *Perceptual and Motor Skills* 76 (1993)

Persinger, M.A., and K. Makarec. "Complex Partial Epileptic Signs as a Continuum from Normals to Epileptics: Normative Data and Clinical Populations." *Journal of Clinical Psychology* 49/1 (January 1993)

Persinger, M.A., et al. "Differential Ratings of Pleasantness Following Right- and Left-Hemispheric Application of Low-Energy Magnetic Fields That Stimulate Long-Term Potentiation." *International Journal of Neuroscience* 70 (1994)

Pidduck, J., Column. *The Mirror*, August 20, 1992

Piehl, A.M., and J.J. Dilulio. "Does Prison Pay?" *The Brookings Review*, Winter 1995

Polsby, D.D. "The False Promise of Gun Control." *The Atlantic Monthly*, March 1994

Prothrow-Stith, D. "Can Physicians Help Curb Adolescent Violence?" *Hospital Practice*, June 15, 1992

Raichle, M.E. "Visualizing the Mind." *Scientific American*, April 1994

Regush, N. "Brain Storms and Angels." *Equinox*, July/August 1995

Rideau, W. "Why Prisons Don't Work." *Time*, March 21, 1994

Rossi, A. "A Biosocial Perspective on Parenting." *Daedalus*, 106 (1977)

————. "The Biosocial Side of Parenthood." *Human Nature*, 1 (1978)

————. "Gender and Parenthood." *American Sociological Review*, 49 (1984)

Sereny, G. "The Truth." *The Independent on Sunday*, February 13, 1994

Simonds, M. "Code of Arms." *Canadian Geographic*, March/April 1996

Smith, D.J. "Little Devils." *The Sunday New York Times*, November 28, 1993

Smith, S.E. "A Test of Possible Cognitive and Environmental Influences on the Mood-Lowering Effect of Tryptophan Depletion in Normal Males." *Psychopharmacology* 91 (1987)

Spivak, H., et al. "Dying Is No Accident." *The Pediatric Clinics of North America* 35/6 (December 1988)

Tardiff, K. "The Current State of Psychiatry in the Treatment of Violent Patients." *Archives of General Psychiatry* 49 (June 1992)

Todd, J. "Feeling Outrage: We Yearn for Harsh Laws to Punish Savage Crimes." *The Gazette*, November 6, 1993

Toffler, A., and H. Toffler. "Getting Set for the Coming Millennium." *The Futurist*, March/April 1995

Walsh, M.W. "Chill Hits Canada's Porn Law." *The Los Angeles Times*, September 6, 1993

Weiss, P. "A Hoplophobe Among the Gunnies." *The New York Times Magazine*, September 11, 1994

Wilson, M., and M. Daly. "Competitiveness, Risk-taking and Violence." *Ethnology and Sociobiology*, 6/59 (1985)

Winkler, M. "Walking Prisons: The Developing Technology of Electronic Controls." *The Futurist*, July/August 1993

Young, S.A., et al. "The Effect of Altered Tryptophan Levels on Mood and Behavior in Normal Males." *Clinical Neuropharmacology* 2, supplement 1 (1988)

Young, S.N., et al. "Biochemical Aspects of Tryptophan Depletion in Primates." *Psychopharmacology* 98 (1989)

Index

Breggin, Peter, 35–36, 37–38, 42, 48, 49, 53, 54, 55, 71, 163–64
Britain, 15, 130–31, 144
British Board of Film Classification, 130
Britton, Paul, 15–16, 17
Bronx Veterans Administration Hospital, 102
Brunner, Han, 40–41
Buddhism, 19
Bulger, James, 15–18, 26, 130, 131
Byers, Patsy Ann, 134

California Supreme Court, 105
Calley, William Laws, Jr., 29–30
Canada:
    censorship in, 131–32
    child poverty in, 170
    crime rates, 140, 151, 159
    gun ownership in, 143, 151–52
    pornography legislation in, 108–9
    prison statistics, 158
Canadian Association of Broadcasters, 132
Canadian Charter of Rights and Freedoms, 108
Canadian Radio-television and
    Telecommunications Commission, 131–32
Capone, Al, 146
Carnegie Corporation, 88
castration, 103, 104
censorship, 130–32, 142, 177
Center for Media Education (Washington), 137
Center for the Study of Psychiatry
    (Bethesda), 36
Centers for Disease Control and Prevention
    (Atlanta), 146, 160
Centerwell, Brandon, 140
cerebellum, 58
cerebrum, 58
Challenge of Anthropology, The (Fox), 82
Chesler, Phyllis, 99
child abuse, 27, 91–92, 94, 112, 116, 118, 120, 162
child pornography, 107
child sex abuse, 101, 102–4, 105, 106, 112–13
children (*See also* child abuse; child porno-
    graphy; child sex abuse)
    aggression in, 15–18, 46, 66, 69, 88, 89–90, 93, 113, 139–40, 166–67, 170
    consumerism and, 135, 136, 139
    exposure to media and, 46, 88, 133, 138–4, 167
    living in poverty, statistics, 170
    Nazi extermination of, 44
chimpanzees, 47, 54, 60
Chimpanzees of Gombe: Patterns of Behavior
    (Goodall), 47
China, 19, 171
chromosomes, 38, 39, 40
Church of Scientology, 55

Churchland, Patricia, 24, 167–68
cingulate gyrus, 60
Clarke Institute of Psychiatry (Toronto), 100–1, 103
"Classified Ad Rapist," 113–14
Cleveland Elementary School (Stockton, California), 117–18
cocaine, 64, 92
Communications Decency Act (1996),132
Comprehensive Psychology, 74
concealed weapons, 148, 149
concentration camps, 44
conditioning, 22–23, 46
Confucius, 19
consciousness:
    mind/body dualism and, 57, 164
    neurologic theories of, 23, 61–62, 23–25, 164, 175
    pathological, 101–2
consumer culture, 130, 135–36, 137, 139
Conyers, John, 33
cooperative living, 23, 82–83, 167, 174
corpus callosum, 58, 86, 87
cortex, 58, 59, 60, 62, 64, 86, 96, 102, 115
"crack" cocaine, 92
Crichton, Michael, 55
Crick, Sir Francis, 23, 84
crime:
    common response to. *See* law-and-orderism;
        social vengeance
    consumerism and, 130, 135–36
    future of, 31, 89, 95, 137, 153, 159, 168–74
    genetics and, 32, 35, 36–42, 48, 114, 164
    gun ownership and, 143–53
    immigration and, 43
    in inner city, 33, 34, 35, 49, 64, 67, 88–89, 144, 163, 166
    media coverage of, 16–17, 26–27, 89, 109, 159
    poverty and, 35, 36, 49, 53, 56, 65, 66, 76, 88–89, 92, 141, 147, 148, 163, 166–67, 170
    racism and, 33, 34, 35, 56, 125, 163, 165
    in schools, 88
    sexual, 96–125
    unemployment and, 35, 49, 88–89, 147, 170
crime statistics:
    assault, 27
    child abuse, 91–92, 102
    drug offenses, 157
    gun-related felonies, 144
    juvenile offenses, 33
    murder, 27, 33, 91, 92, 95, 111, 140–41, 144, 151, 158, 159
    rape, 27, 97
cryptopyrrole, 114
cultural anthropology, 44–45